CAMBRIDGE STUDIES IN PHILOSOPHY

The Theory and Practice of Autonomy

CAMBRIDGE STUDIES IN PHILOSOPHY

General editor SYDNEY SHOEMAKER

Advisory editors J. E. J. ALTHAM, SIMON BLACKBURN,
GILBERT HARMAN, MARTIN HOLLIS, FRANK JACKSON,
JONATHAN LEAR, JOHN PERRY, BARRY STROUD

The Theory and Practice of Autonomy

Gerald Dworkin
University of Illinois at Chicago

The right of the
University of Cambridge
to print and sell
all manner of books
was granted by
Henry VIII in 1534.
The University has printed
and published continuously
since 1584.

Cambridge University Press

Cambridge

New York   New Rochelle   Melbourne   Sydney

Published by the Press Syndicate of the University of Cambridge
The Pitt Building, Trumpington Street, Cambridge CB2 1RP
32 East 57th Street, New York, NY 10022, USA
10 Stamford Road, Oakleigh, Melbourne 3166, Australia

First published 1988

Printed in the United States of America

Library of Congress Cataloging-in-Publication Data
Dworkin, Gerald.
The theory and practice of autonomy / Gerald Dworkin.
p.   cm. – (Cambridge studies in philosophy)
ISBN 0-521-34452-2.   ISBN 0-521-35767-5 (pbk.)
1. Ethics.   2. Autonomy.   I. Title.   II. Series.
BJ1031.D86   1988
170 – dc19   87-32554
CIP

British Library Cataloguing in Publication Data
Dworkin, Gerald
The theory and practice of autonomy. –
(Cambridge studies in philosophy).
1. Liberty
I. Title
123'.5   JC585

ISBN 0 521 34452 2 hard covers
ISBN 0 521 35767 5 paperback

For
Miriam, who made it possible
Joan, who made it probable

Contents

Preface

I

There are those who know from the start where they are going and those who only realize after the journey where they have been traveling. I am one of the latter. I wrote about issues, problems, theses, as they occurred to me, as they provoked or baffled me, *seriatim*. My Ph.D. thesis was on the nature and justification of coercion, and two of my earliest publications were based on that work.[1] In one I considered why those who choose under coercive pressures should not be considered to be acting freely (in spite of the fact that they would prefer to choose as they do, given their circumstances). In the other I considered the kinds of interferences with people justified by reference to their own good and when, if ever, such interferences might be justified. In both cases I was dealing with the choices people make and the significance and value of their making those choices in accordance with their own standards and preferences. I had embarked, without being aware of it, on a voyage circling that territory which I later came to think of as "autonomy."

My first actual use of the term was in an essay in applied ethics.[2] It was written at a time when there was much concern about issues such as psychosurgery, aversive conditioning, subliminal advertising, and drug therapy. I was asked by the Hastings Center to participate in a working group considering the ethics of various ways of influencing persons and their behavior. I realized that many claims were made about the ethical significance of various techniques in terms of their differential effects on autonomy, but that very little was said about that elusive concept. I embarked on my first exploration into the territory itself.

1 "Acting Freely," *Nous* (November 1970). "Paternalism," *Monist* (January 1972).
2 "Autonomy and Behavior Control," *Hastings Center Report* (February 1976).

ix

In the succeeding years there were reasons of a theoretical and practical nature for my continued interest in the topic. This was a decade in which bioethics was rapidly developing, and one of its central problems was that of medical experimentation and innovative therapy. Discussions of informed consent, of proxy consent, of prisoners as subjects of experimentation, of drug testing on children, all required that attention be paid to the nature and value of autonomy. This was also a period in which the traditional doctor–patient relationship, based on "doctor knows best" paternalism, was undergoing a fundamental shift to a more contractualist basis. Issues of paternalism also arose with respect to such public policy issues as in-kind welfare payments, social security, the banning of laetrile, and seat-belt legislation. Why, and under what conditions, we should restrict people's autonomy in their own best interests remains a crucial issue of public policy.

There were also reasons of a theoretical nature for continued interest in the topic of autonomy. Shortly after my article "Acting Freely" had come out, Harry Frankfurt had published his extremely influential article "Freedom of the Will and the Concept of a Person."[3] The theory put forward there, like mine a hierarchical structure, stimulated a large literature concerning the conceptual merits and plausibility of such a theory. At the same time the Kantian and neo-Kantian reaction to utilitarianism was developing, and one of the two central normative concepts was that of autonomy – the other being "respect." It soon became apparent, however, that autonomy was being used (in both senses) in a rather vague and excessively broad fashion. The concept of autonomy required the same kind of care and detailed mapping that ideas such as liberty and equality had received at the hands of earlier philosophers.

II

Chapter 1 develops a notion of autonomy which meets various conceptual and normative constraints that are set prior to the analysis of the concept. Chapter 2 examines various issues concerning the value of the conception set out in Chapter 1. Chapters 3 and 4 extend the discussion from a very general idea of autonomy to the

---

3 "Freedom of the Will and the Concept of a Person," *Journal of Philosophy* 68 (January 1971).

notion discussed by philosophers and others under the heading of moral autonomy. They raise the issue of whether autonomy has a rather different status in our moral life than in other spheres, such as the natural sciences, and whether, and to what extent, moral autonomy ought to be valued. Chapter 5 is addressed to a similar issue concerning the range of choices available to us: Is it always a good thing to have a wider rather narrower range of options from which to choose?

The essays in Part II apply the general framework developed in Part I to various concrete moral questions. These include informed consent to experimental and therapeutic interventions, what to do when persons are too young or not competent to give informed consent, and some further reflections on what kinds of interventions count as paternalistic and the conditions for justification of such interference. Finally there are two essays on more general issues of public policy involving choice: the use of entrapment by law-enforcement officials and whether it is better for a society to try to plan and design its institutions rather than let them develop in less self-conscious ways.

I have not included two essays ("Paternalism" and "Autonomy and Behavior Control") because both have been widely reprinted and because the views expressed in them have undergone considerable revision – particularly those in the latter essay.

Acknowledgments

Newton said that if he saw further than others it was because he stood on the shoulders of giants. If he had stood on the shoulders of midgets he would also have seen further. Any elevation helps. If I have seen any further it's because I have stood on the shoulders of many persons who were willing to provide aid, encouragement, and wisdom. Many of them are acknowledged in individual essays, but I would like to express my particular gratitude to Tom Nagel, who started me off on the path that led to this book.

Institutions have played their part as well. The Hastings Center provided me with time and intellectual stimulation as a Luce Senior Scholar. The Humanities Institute at the University of Illinois at Chicago did the same. Eileen Iverson provided valuable secretarial assistance in the production of the finished manuscript.

PART I

Theory

1

The nature of autonomy

I

The concept of autonomy has assumed increasing importance in contemporary moral and political philosophy. Philosophers such as John Rawls, Thomas Scanlon, Robert P. Wolff, and Ronald Dworkin have employed the concept to define and illuminate issues such as the characterization of principles of justice, the limits of free speech, and the nature of the liberal state.

In the most recent formulation of the foundations of his theory of justice, Rawls makes clear – what was implicit in his book – that a certain ideal of the person is the cornerstone of his moral edifice. A central feature of that idea is the notion of autonomy.

> [T]he main idea of Kantian constructivism . . . is to establish a connection between the first principles of justice and the conception of moral persons as free and equal. . . . [T]he requisite connection is provided by a procedure of construction in which rationally autonomous agents subject to reasonable constraints agree to public principles of justice.[1]

Scanlon's defense of a Millian principle of free speech relies also on a view of what powers autonomous persons would grant to the state.

> I will defend the Millian principle by showing it to be a consequence of the view that the powers of a state are limited to those that citizens could recognize while still regarding themselves as equal, autonomous, rational agents.[2]

Portions of this chapter were originally published in *GRAZER Philosophische Studien* 12/13 (1981), 203–13. Reprinted by permission.

1 John Rawls, "Construction and Objectivity," *Journal of Philosophy* 78 (September 1980), 554.
2 Thomas Scanlon, "A Theory of Freedom of Expression," *Philosophy and Public Affairs* 1 (Winter 1972), 215.

Ronald Dworkin, in his article on Liberalism, does not use the word "autonomy," but in discussing the idea of treating people as equals he is arguing for equal respect for the autonomy of citizens.

According to Dworkin, the liberal theory of equality supposes that political decisions must be, so far as is possible, independent of any particular conception of the good life, or of what gives value to life. Since the citizens of a society differ in their conceptions, the government does not treat them as equals if it prefers one conception to another, either because the officials believe that one is intrinsically superior or because it is held by the more numerous or more powerful group.[3]

Wolff's essay, *In Defense of Anarchism*, is devoted to the task of demonstrating that a citizen cannot retain his autonomy and at the same time be under an obligation to obey the commands of the state simply because they are the commands of the state.

> The autonomous ... man may do what another tells him, but not because he has been told to do it ... by accepting as final the commands of the others, he forfeits his autonomy ... a promise to abide by the will of the majority creates an obligation, but it does so precisely by giving up one's autonomy.[4]

Bruce Ackerman, in his *Social Justice in the Liberal State*, speaks of

> respect for the autonomy of persons as one of the four main highways to the liberal state. ... It is, in short, not necessary for autonomy to be the only good thing; it suffices for it to be the best thing that there is.[5]

It is clear that either as interpretations of the idea of liberty and equality, or as additions to them, the notion of autonomy plays a central role in current normative philosophical work. It is also apparent that, unlike the concepts of liberty and equality, it has not received careful and comprehensive philosophical examination.

Proceeding simultaneously, and as far as I can tell, relatively independently, the idea of autonomy has emerged as a central notion in the area of applied moral philosophy, particularly in the biomed-

---

3 Ronald Dworkin, "Liberalism," in *Public and Private Morality*, ed. S. Hampshire (Cambridge: Cambridge University Press, 1978), 127.
4 Robert Paul Wolff, *In Defense of Anarchism* (New York: Harper & Row, 1970), 14, 41.
5 Bruce Ackerman, *Social Justice in the Liberal State* (New Haven: Yale University Press, 1980), 368–69.

4

ical context. All discussions of the nature of informed consent and its rationale refer to patient (or subject) autonomy. Conflicts between autonomy and paternalism occur in cases involving civil commitment, lying to patients, refusals of life-saving treatment, suicide intervention, and patient care.

Whether or not this is the same concept that appears in the more theoretical discussions remains to be seen, but we have some reason to believe that philosophical scrutiny will be of more than just theoretical interest.

One more warning by way of introduction. It would be unwise to assume that different authors are all referring to the same thing when they use the term "autonomy." By way of illustration, consider the following brief catalogue of uses of the term in moral and political philosophy.

[T]he law in thus implementing its basic commitment to man's autonomy, his freedom to and his freedom from, acknowledge(s) how complex man is.[6]

To regard himself as autonomous in the sense I have in mind, a person must see himself as sovereign in deciding what to believe and in weighing competing reasons for action.[7]

As Kant argued, moral autonomy is a combination of freedom and responsibility; it is a submission to laws that one has made for oneself. The autonomous man, insofar as he is autonomous, is not subject to the will of another.[8]

(Children) finally pass to the level of autonomy when they appreciate that rules are alterable, that they can be criticized and should be accepted or rejected on a basis of reciprocity and fairness. The emergence of rational reflection about rules . . . central to the Kantian conception of autonomy, is the main feature of the final level of moral development.[9]

I am autonomous if I rule me, and no one else rules I.[10]

6 Joseph Goldstein, "On being Adult and Being an Adult in Secular Law," in *Adulthood*, ed. E. H. Erikson (New York: W. W. Norton and Co., 1978), 252.
7 Thomas Scanlon, "A Theory of Freedom of Expression," *Philosophy and Public Affairs* 1 (1972), 215.
8 Robert Paul Wolff, *In Defense of Anarchism* (New York: Harper & Row, 1970), 14.
9 R. S. Peters, "Freedom and the Development of the Free Man," in *Education and the Development of Reason*, ed. R. F. Dearden (London: Routledge and Kegan Paul, 1972), 130.
10 Joel Feinberg, "The Idea of a Free Man," in *Education and the Development of Reason*, 161.

Human beings are commonly spoken of as autonomous creatures. We have suggested that their autonomy consists in their ability to choose whether to think in a certain way insofar as thinking is acting; in their freedom from obligation within certain spheres of life; and in their moral individuality.[11]

A person is "autonomous" to the degree that what he thinks and does cannot be explained without reference to his own activity of mind.[12]

[A]cting autonomously is acting from principles that we would consent to as free and equal rational beings.[13]

I, and I alone, am ultimately responsible for the decisions I make, and am in that sense autonomous.[14]

It is apparent that, although not used just as a synonym for qualities that are usually approved of, "autonomy" is used in an exceedingly broad fashion. It is used sometimes as an equivalent of liberty (positive or negative in Berlin's terminology), sometimes as equivalent to self-rule or sovereignty, sometimes as identical with freedom of the will. It is equated with dignity, integrity, individuality, independence, responsibility, and self-knowledge. It is identified with qualities of self-assertion, with critical reflection, with freedom from obligation, with absence of external causation, with knowledge of one's own interests. It is even equated by some economists with the impossibility of interpersonal comparisons. It is related to actions, to beliefs, to reasons for acting, to rules, to the will of other persons, to thoughts, and to principles. About the only features held constant from one author to another are that autonomy is a feature of persons and that it is a desirable quality to have.

It is very unlikely that there is a core meaning which underlies all these various uses of the term. Autonomy is a term of art and will not repay an Austinian investigation of its ordinary uses. It will be necessary to construct a concept given various theoretical purposes and some constraints from normal usage.

11 R. S. Downie, Elizabeth Telfer, "Autonomy," *Philosophy* 15 (1971), 301.
12 R. F. Dearden, "Autonomy and Education," in *Education and the Development of Reason*, ed. R. F. Dearden, (London: Routledge and Kegan Paul, 1972), 453.
13 John Rawls, *A Theory of Justice* (Cambridge: Harvard University Press, 1971), 516.
14 J. L. Lucas, *Principles of Politics* (Oxford University Press, 1966), 101.

II

I shall begin by discussing the nature of autonomy. Given various problems that may be clarified or resolved with the aid of a concept of autonomy, how may we most usefully characterize the concept? I use the vague term "characterize" rather than "define" or "analyze" because I do not think it possible with any moderately complex philosophical concept to specify necessary and sufficient conditions without draining the concept of the very complexity that enables it to perform its theoretical role. Autonomy is a term of art introduced by a theorist in an attempt to make sense of a tangled net of intuitions, conceptual and empirical issues, and normative claims. What one needs, therefore, is a study of how the term is connected with other notions, what role it plays in justifying various normative claims, how the notion is supposed to ground ascriptions of value, and so on – in short, a theory.

A theory, however, requires conditions of adequacy; constraints we impose antecedently on any satisfactory development of the concept. In the absence of some theoretical, empirical, or normative limits, we have no way of arguing for or against any proposed explication. To say this is not to deny the possibility we may end up some distance from our starting point. The difficulties we encounter may best be resolved by adding or dropping items from the initial set of constraints. But without some limits to run up against, we are too free to make progress.

I propose the following criteria for a satisfactory theory of autonomy:

Logical consistency. The concept should be neither internally inconsistent nor inconsistent (logically) with other concepts we know to be consistent. So, for example, if the idea of an uncaused cause were inconsistent and autonomy required the existence of such a cause, it would fail to satisfy this criterion.

Empirical possibility. There should be no empirically grounded or theoretically derived knowledge which makes it impossible or extremely unlikely that anybody ever has been, or could be, autonomous. Thus, a theory which required as a condition of autonomy that an individual's values not be influenced by his parents, peers, or culture would violate this condition. It is important to note that this condition is not designed to beg the question (in the long run) against those, such as Skinner, who deny the possibility of autonomy. I am attempting to construct a notion of autonomy that is empirically possible. I may fail. This might be due to my limitations. If enough people fail, the best explanation may be that Skinner is correct. Or he may be correct about certain explications and not others. It would then be important to determine whether the ones that are not possible are the ones that are significant for moral and political questions.

We see here how the constraints operate as a system. It would not be legitimate to reject a proposed explication of autonomy on the grounds that we know that nobody is autonomous in that sense if *that* sense were the very one people have appealed to when deriving normative claims.

Value conditions. It should be explicable on the basis of the theory why, at the least, people have thought that being autonomous was a desirable state of affairs. A strong constraint would require that the theory show why autonomy is not merely thought to be a good, but why it is a good. A still stronger constraint would require that the theory show why, as Kant claimed, autonomy is the supreme good. Because I do not intend my theory as an explication of Kant's views, and because it is plausible to suppose that there are competing values which may, on occasion, outweigh that of autonomy, I do not adopt the strongest constraint.

As an additional constraint I suggest that the theory not imply a logical incompatibility with other significant values, that is, that the autonomous person not be ruled out on conceptual grounds from manifesting other virtues or acting justly.

Ideological neutrality. I intend by this a rather weak constraint. The concept should be one that has value for very different ideological outlooks. Thus, it should not be the case that only individualistic ideologies can value autonomy. This is compatible with the claim that various ideologies may differ greatly on the weight to be attached to the value of autonomy, the trade-offs that are reasonable, whether the value be intrinsic, instrumental, and so forth.

Normative relevance. The theory should make intelligible the philosophical uses of the concept. One should see why it is plausible

8

to use the concept to ground a principle protecting freedom of speech, or why Rawls uses the idea of autonomous persons as part of a contractual argument for certain principles of distributive justice. One may also use the theory in a critical fashion to argue that a theory which argues from a notion of autonomy to the denial of legitimate state authority has gone wrong because it uses too strong a notion of autonomy.

Judgmental relevance. The final constraint is that the explication of the concept be in general accord with particular judgments we make about autonomy. These judgments may be conceptual: for example, one may believe that autonomy is not an all-or-nothing concept but a matter of more or less. The judgments may be normative, for example that autonomy is that value against which paternalism offends. The judgments may be empirical, for example that the only way to promote autonomy in adults is to allow them as children a considerable and increasing degree of autonomy.

I do not believe, however, that one can set out in advance a "privileged" set of judgments which must be preserved. If the judgments do not hang together, then any of them may have to be hanged separately.

These are the criteria. It is possible that no concept of autonomy satisfies them all. Just as Kenneth Arrow discovered there was no social welfare function satisfying certain plausible constraints, we may find there is no concept satisfying ours. That itself would be an interesting discovery and would raise the question of whether we ought to drop or weaken some of the constraints or, perhaps, abandon the idea of autonomy.

What is more likely is that there is no single conception of autonomy but that we have one concept and many conceptions of autonomy – to make use of a distinction first introduced by H.L.A. Hart and developed by Rawls. The concept is an abstract notion that specifies in very general terms the role the concept plays. Thus, a certain idea of persons as self-determining is shared by very different philosophical positions. Josiah Royce speaks of a person as a life led according to a plan. Marxists speak of man as the creature who makes himself; existentialists of a being whose being is always in question; Kantians of persons making law for themselves. At a very abstract level I believe they share the same concept of autonomy. But when it comes to specifying more concretely what prin-

9

ciples justify interference with autonomy, what is the nature of the "self" which does the choosing, what the connections between autonomy and dependence on others are, then there will be different and conflicting views on these matters. This filling out of an abstract concept with different content is what is meant by different conceptions of the same concept.

I intend to present a view that provides specifications for most of these questions, but since I believe that the value of a particular conception is always relative to a set of problems and questions, I want first to indicate the range of issues that I see as relevant to the conception I shall develop.

Autonomy functions as a moral, political, and social ideal. In all three cases there is value attached to how things are viewed through the reasons, values, and desires of the individual and how those elements are shaped and formed.

As a political ideal, autonomy is used as a basis to argue against the design and functioning of political institutions that attempt to impose a set of ends, values, and attitudes upon the citizens of a society. This imposition might be based on a theological view, or secular visions of a good society, or on the importance of achieving excellence along some dimension of human achievement. In each case the argument favoring such imposition is made independently of the value of the institutions as viewed by each citizen. Those favoring autonomy urge that the process of justification of political institutions must be acceptable to each citizen, must appeal to considerations that are recognized to be valid by all the members of the society.

In particular, then, autonomy is used to oppose perfectionist or paternalistic views. It is also related to what Ronald Dworkin refers to as the notion of equal respect. A government is required to treat its citizens neutrally, in the sense that it cannot favor the interests of some over others. This idea is used by Dworkin to argue for the existence of various rights.

Conceptions of autonomy are also used, by Wolff and others, to argue for the illegitimacy of obedience to authority. The emphasis in this argument is on the individual making up his own mind about the merits of legal restrictions. This use of autonomy seems much closer in content to the ideal of moral autonomy. As a moral notion – shared by philosophers as divergent as Kant, Kierkegaard, Nietzsche, Royce, Hare, and Popper – the argument is about the

10

necessity or desirability of individuals choosing or willing or accepting their own moral code. We are all responsible for developing and criticizing our moral principles, and individual conscience must take precedence over authority and tradition. I am not defending this line of reasoning, but it is certainly a body of thought which makes use of the notion of autonomy and has a corresponding set of problems connected with responsibility, integrity, and the will.[15] A theory of autonomy must throw some light on these problems, even if it does not accept (all of) the proposed solutions.

Finally, we have a set of issues concerning the ways in which the nonpolitical institutions of a society affect the values, attitudes, and beliefs of the members of the society. Our dispositions, attitudes, values, wants are affected by the economic institutions, by the mass media, by the force of public opinion, by social class, and so forth. To a large extent these institutions are not chosen by us; we simply find ourselves faced with them. From Humboldt, Mill, and DeTocqueville to Marcuse and Reismann, social theorists have worried about how individuals can develop their own conception of the good life in the face of such factors, and how we can distinguish between legitimate and illegitimate ways of influencing the minds of the members of society.

While Marxists have been most vocal in raising the issues of "false consciousness," and "true versus false needs," it is important to see that the question is one which a wide range of social theorists must address. For it is a reasonable feature of any good society that it is self-sustaining in the sense that people who grow up in such a society will acquire a respect for and commitment to the principles which justify and regulate its existence. It is very unlikely that the development of such dispositions is something over which individuals have much control or choice. Socialization into the norms and values of the society will have taken place at a very young age. It looks, then, as if we can only distinguish between institutions on the basis of what they convey, their content, and not on the basis that they influence people at a stage when they cannot be critical about such matters. It looks, therefore, as if autonomy in the acquisition of principles and values is impossible.

In all three areas – moral, political, social – we find that there is a notion of the self which is to be respected, left unmanipulated,

15 See chaps. 3 and 4.

11

and which is, in certain ways, independent and self-determining. But we also find certain tensions and paradoxes. If the notion of self-determination is given a very strong definition – the unchosen chooser, the uninfluenced influencer – then it seems as if autonomy is impossible. We know that all individuals have a history. They develop socially and psychologically in a given environment with a set of biological endowments. They mature slowly and are, therefore, heavily influenced by parents, peers, and culture. How, then, can we talk of self-determination?

Again, there seems to be a conflict between self-determination and notions of correctness and objectivity. If we are to make reasonable choices, then we must be governed by canons of reasoning, norms of conduct, standards of excellence that are not themselves the products of our choices. We have acquired them at least partly as the result of others' advice, example, teaching – or, perhaps, by some innate coding. In any case, we cannot have determined these for ourselves.[16]

Finally, there is a tension between autonomy as a purely formal notion (where what one decides for oneself can have any particular content), and autonomy as a substantive notion (where only certain decisions count as retaining autonomy whereas others count as forfeiting it). So the person who decides to do what his community, or guru, or comrades tells him to do cannot on the latter view count as autonomous. Autonomy then seems in conflict with emotional ties to others, with commitments to causes, with authority, tradition, expertise, leadership, and so forth.

What I shall try to do now is introduce a conception of autonomy that satisfies the criteria set out at the beginning and that is (1) relevant to the moral, political, and social issues mentioned above; (2) possible to achieve; and (3) able to avoid the difficulties and problems just enumerated.

III

The central idea that underlies the concept of autonomy is indicated by the etymology of the term: *autos* (self) and *nomos* (rule or law). The term was first applied to the Greek city state. A city had

16 See chap. 4.

autonomia when its citizens made their own laws, as opposed to being under the control of some conquering power.

There is then a natural extension to persons as being autonomous when their decisions and actions are their own; when they are self-determining. The impetus for this extension occurs first when questions of following one's conscience are raised by religious thinkers. Aquinas, Luther, and Calvin placed great stress on the individual acting in accordance with reason as shaped and perceived by the person. This idea is then taken up by the Renaissance humanists. Pico della Mirandola expresses the idea clearly in his "Oration on the Dignity of Man." God says to Adam:

> We have given thee, Adam, no fixed seat, no form of thy very own, no gift peculiarly thine, that . . . thou mayest . . . possess as thine own the seat, the form, the gift which thou thyself shalt desire . . . thou wilt fix the limits of thy nature for thyself . . . thou . . . art the molder and the maker of thyself.[17]

The same concept is presented by Berlin under the heading of "positive liberty":

> I wish to be an instrument of my own, not other men's acts of will. I wish to be a subject, not an object . . . deciding, not being decided for, self-directed and not acted upon by external nature or by other men as if I were a thing, or an animal, or a slave incapable of playing a human role, that is, of conceiving goals and policies of my own and realizing them.[18]

But this abstract concept only can be understood as particular specifications are made of the notions of "self," "my own," "internal," and so forth. Is it the noumenal self of Kant, or the historical self of Marx? Which mode of determination (choice, decision, invention, consent) is singled out? At what level is autonomy centered – individual decision, rule, values, motivation? Is autonomy a global or a local concept? Is it predicated of relatively long stretches of an individual's life or relatively brief ones?

Let me begin by considering the relationship between the liberty or freedom of an individual and his autonomy. Are these two distinct notions? Are they linked, perhaps, in hierarchical fashion so that, say, interference with liberty is always interference with

---

17 Quoted in P. O. Kristeller, "The Philosophy of Man in the Italian Renaissance," *Italica* 24 (1947), 100–1.
18 I. Berlin, *Four Essays on Liberty* (Oxford: Oxford University Press, 1969), 131.

autonomy, but not vice-versa? Are they, perhaps, merely syn-onymous?

Suppose we think of liberty as being, roughly, the ability of a person to do what she wants, to have (significant) options that are not closed or made less eligible by the actions of other agents. Then the typical ways of interfering with the liberty of an agent (coercion and force) seem to also interfere with her autonomy (thought of, for the moment, as a power of self-determination). If we force a Jehovah's Witness to have a blood transfusion, this not only is a direct interference with his liberty, but also a violation of his ability to determine for himself what kinds of medical treatment are ac-ceptable to him. Patient autonomy *is* the ability of patients to decide on courses of treatment, to choose particular physicians, and so forth.

But autonomy cannot be identical to liberty for, when we deceive a patient, we are also interfering with her autonomy. Deception is not a way of restricting liberty. The person who, to use Locke's example, is put into a cell and convinced that all the doors are locked (when, in fact, one is left unlocked) is free to leave the cell. But because he cannot – given his information – avail himself of this opportunity, his ability to do what he wishes is limited. Self-determination can be limited in other ways than by interferences with liberty.

Both coercion and deception infringe upon the voluntary char-acter of the agent's actions. In both cases a person will feel used, will see herself as an instrument of another's will. Her actions, although in one sense hers because she did them, are in another sense attributable to another. It is because of this that such infringe-ments may excuse or (partially) relieve a person of responsibility for what she has done. The normal links between action and char-acter are broken when action is involuntary.

Why, then, should we not restrict our categories to those of freedom, ignorance, and voluntariness? Why do we need a separate notion of autonomy? One reason is because not every interference with the voluntary character of one's action interferes with a per-son's ability to choose his mode of life. If, as is natural, we focus only on cases where the person wishes to be free from interference, resents having his liberty interfered with, we miss an important dimension of a person's actions.

Consider the classic case of Odysseus. Not wanting to be lured onto the rocks by the sirens, he commands his men to tie him to the mast and refuse all later orders he will give to be set free. He wants to have his freedom limited so that he can survive. Although his behavior at the time he hears the sirens may not be voluntary – he struggles against his bonds and orders his men to free him – there is another dimension of his conduct that must be understood. He has a preference about his preferences, a desire not to have or to act upon various desires. He views the desire to move his ship closer to the sirens as something that is no part of him, but alien to him. In limiting his liberty, in accordance with his wishes, we promote, not hinder, his efforts to define the contours of his life.

To consider only the promotion or hindrance of first-order desires – which is what we focus upon in considering the voluntariness of action – is to ignore a crucial feature of persons, their ability to reflect upon and adopt attitudes toward their first-order desires, wishes, intentions.

It is characteristic of persons, and seems to be a distinctively human ability, that they are able to engage in this kind of activity. One may not just desire to smoke, but also desire that one not have that desire. I may not just be motivated by jealousy or anger, but may also desire that my motivations be different (or the same).

A person may identify with the influences that motivate him, assimilate them to himself, view himself as the kind of person who wishes to be moved in particular ways. Or, he may resent being motivated in certain ways, be alienated from those influences, prefer to be the kind of person who is motivated in different ways. In an earlier essay I suggested that it was a necessary condition for being autonomous that a person's second-order identifications be congruent with his first-order motivations.[19] This condition, which I called "authenticity," was to be necessary but not sufficient for being autonomous.

I now believe that this is mistaken. It is not the identification or lack of identification that is crucial to being autonomous, but the capacity to raise the question of whether I will identify with or reject the reasons for which I now act. There are a number of considerations that tell against my earlier view.

First, autonomy seems intuitively to be a global rather than local

19 G. Dworkin, "Autonomy and Behavior Control," *Hastings Center Report* (February 1976).

15

concept. It is a feature that evaluates a whole way of living one's life and can only be assessed over extended portions of a person's life, whereas identification is something that may be pinpointed over short periods of time. We can think of a person who today identifies with, say, his addiction, but tomorrow feels it as alien and who continues to shift back and forth at frequent intervals. Does he shift back and forth from autonomy to nonautonomy?

Second, identification does not seem to be what is put in question by obvious interferences with autonomy. The person who is kept ignorant or who is lobotomized or who is manipulated in various ways (all obvious interferences with autonomy) is not having his identifications interfered with, but rather his capacity or ability either to make or reject such identifications.

Third, there seems to be an implication of the position that is counterintuitive. Suppose that there is a conflict between one's second-order desires and one's first-order desires. Say one is envious but does not want to be an envious person. One way of becoming autonomous is by ceasing to be motivated by envy. But another way, on the view being considered here, is to change one's objections to envy, to change one's second-order preferences.

Now there may be certain limits on the ways this can be done that are spelled out in the other necessary condition which I elaborated: that of procedural independence. So, for example, it wouldn't do to have oneself hypnotized into identifying with one's envious motivations. But even if the procedures used were "legitimate," there seems to be something wrong with the idea that one becomes more autonomous by changing one's higher-order preferences.

Fourth, this view breaks the link between the idea of autonomy and the ability to make certain desires effective in our actions. On this view, the drug addict who desires to be motivated by his addiction, and yet who cannot change his behavior, is autonomous because his actions express his view of what influences he wants to be motivating him. This seems too passive a view. Autonomy should have some relationship to the ability of individuals, not only to scrutinize critically their first-order motivations but also to change them if they so desire. Obviously the requirement cannot be as strong as the notion that "at will" a person can change his first-order preferences. Indeed, there are certain sorts of inabilities of this nature that are perfectly compatible with autonomy. A person who cannot affect his desires to act justly or compassionately is not thought by that fact alone to be nonautonomous. Perhaps there is still the idea that if justice were not a virtue or that if, in a given case, hardness and not compassion were required, the agent could adjust his desires. Susan Wolf has suggested the requirement that a person "could have done otherwise if there had been good and sufficient reason."[20]

The idea of autonomy is not merely an evaluative or reflective notion, but includes as well some ability both to alter one's preferences and to make them effective in one's actions and, indeed, to make them effective because one has reflected upon them and adopted them as one's own.

It is important both to guard against certain intellectualist conceptions of autonomy as well as to be candid about the ways in which people may differ in their actual exercise of autonomy. The first error would be to suppose that my views imply that only certain types or classes of people can be autonomous. If we think of the process of reflection and identification as being a conscious, fully articulated, and explicit process, then it will appear that it is mainly professors of philosophy who exercise autonomy and that those who are less educated, or who are by nature or upbringing less reflective, are not, or not as fully, autonomous individuals. But a farmer living in an isolated rural community, with a minimal education, may without being aware of it be conducting his life in ways which indicate that he has shaped and molded his life according to reflective procedures. This will be shown not by what he says about his thoughts, but in what he tries to change in his life, what he criticizes about others, the satisfaction he manifests (or fails to) in his work, family, and community.

It may be true, however, that there is empirical and theoretical evidence that certain personality types, or certain social classes, or certain cultures are more (or less) likely to exercise their capacity to be autonomous. I do not suppose that the actual exercise of this capacity is less subject to empirical determination than, say, the virtue of courage. To the extent that this is borne out by the evidence, we must be on guard against the tendency to attribute greater value to characteristics which are more likely to be found in twentieth-century intellectuals than in other groups or cultures.

20 S. Wolf, "Asymmetric Freedom," *Journal of Philosophy* 77 (1980), 159.

To return to our original question of the relation between autonomy and liberty, I would claim that the two are distinct notions, but related in both contingent and noncontingent ways. Normally persons wish to act freely. So, interfering with a person's liberty also interferes with the ways in which he wants to be motivated, the kind of person he wants to be, and hence with his autonomy. But a person who wishes to be restricted in various ways, whether by the discipline of the monastery, regimentation of the army, or even by coercion, is not, on that account alone, less autonomous. Further, I would argue that the condition of being a chooser (where one's choices are not defined by the threats of another) is not just contingently linked to being an autonomous person, but must be the standard case from which exceptions are seen as precisely that – exceptions. Liberty, power, control over important aspects of one's life are not the same as autonomy, but are necessary conditions for individuals to develop their own aims and interests and to make their values effective in the living of their lives.

Second-order reflection cannot be the whole story of autonomy. For those reflections, the choice of the kind of person one wants to become, may be influenced by other persons or circumstances in such a fashion that we do not view those evaluations as being the person's own. In "Autonomy and Behavior Control" I called this a failure of procedural independence.

Spelling out the conditions of procedural independence involves distinguishing those ways of influencing people's reflective and critical faculties which subvert them from those which promote and improve them. It involves distinguishing those influences such as hypnotic suggestion, manipulation, coercive persuasion, subliminal influence, and so forth, and doing so in a non ad hoc fashion. Philosophers interested in the relationships between education and indoctrination, advertising and consumer behavior, and behavior control have explored these matters in some detail, but with no finality.

Finally, I wish to consider two objections that can (and have) been raised to my views.[21] The first is an objection to introducing

21 I am indebted to an unpublished manuscript, "Autonomy and External Influence," of John Christman for his ideas on these points. For further discussion, see Irving Thalberg, "Hierarchical Analyses of Unfree Action," *Canadian Journal of Philosophy* 8 (June 1978) and Marilyn Friedman, "Autonomy and the Split-Level Self," *Southern Journal of Philosophy* 24 (1986, no. 1).

the level of second-order reflection at all. The second is why should we stop at the second level and is an infinite regress not threatened.

The first objection says that we can accomplish all we need to by confining our attention to people's first-order motivation. After all, on my own view of the significance of procedural independence, we have to find a way to make principled distinctions among different ways of influencing our critical reflections, so why not do this directly at the first level. We can distinguish coerced from free acts, manipulated from authentic desires, and so forth. My reply is that I think we fail to capture something important about human agents if we make our distinctions solely at the first level. We need to distinguish not only between the person who is coerced and the person who acts, say, to obtain pleasure, but also between two agents who are coerced. One resents being motivated in this fashion, would not choose to enter situations in which threats are present. The other welcomes being motivated in this fashion, chooses (even pays) to be threatened. A similar contrast holds between two patients, one of whom is deceived by his doctor against his will and the other who has requested that his doctor lie to him if cancer is ever diagnosed. Our normative and conceptual theories would be deficient if the distinction between levels were not drawn.

The second objection is twofold. First, what is particularly significant about the second level? Might we not have preferences about our second-order preferences? Could I not regret the fact that I welcome the fact that I am not sufficiently generous in my actions? I accept this claim, at least in principle. As a theory about the presence or absence of certain psychological states empirical evidence is relevant. It appears that for some agents, and some motivations, there is higher-order reflection. If so, then autonomy will be thought of as the highest-order approval and integration. As a matter of contingent fact human beings either do not, or perhaps cannot, carry on such iteration at great length.

The second part of this objection concerns the acts of critical reflection themselves. Either these acts are themselves autonomous (in which case we have to go to a higher-order reflection to determine this, and since this process can be repeated an infinite regress threatens) or they are not autonomous, in which case why is a first-order motivation evaluated by a nonautonomous process *itself* autonomous. My response to this objection is that I am not trying to analyze the notion of autonomous *acts*, but of what it means to

19

be an autonomous person, to have a certain capacity and exercise it. I do claim that the process of reflection ought to be subject to the requirements of procedural independence, but if a person's reflections have not been manipulated, coerced, and so forth and if the person does have the requisite identification then they are, on my view, autonomous. There is no conceptual necessity for raising the question of whether the values, preferences at the second order would themselves be valued or preferred at a higher level, although in particular cases the agent might engage in such higher-order reflection.

Putting the various pieces together, autonomy is conceived of as a second-order capacity of persons to reflect critically upon their first-order preferences, desires, wishes, and so forth and the capacity to accept or attempt to change these in light of higher-order preferences and values. By exercising such a capacity, persons define their nature, give meaning and coherence to their lives, and take responsibility for the kind of person they are.

2

The value of autonomy

I have outlined a conception of autonomy; a conception that is in various ways different from other conceptions of autonomy that have historically been developed. One way of attacking such a conception is by arguing that it does not fulfill the evaluative tasks that have traditionally been associated with the notion. In this chapter I wish to defend the conception developed in Chapter 1 against a certain attack and then to argue for the value of exercising autonomy when understood in this way.

There is a traditional view of autonomy that must view my conception as too thin to be of value because there is no specific content to the decisions an autonomous person takes. Suppose we have a person who has not been subjected to the kinds of influence – whatever they turn out to be – that interfere with procedural independence. Suppose the person wants to conduct his or her life in accordance with the following: Do whatever my mother or my buddies or my leader or my priest tells me to do. Such a person counts, in my view, as autonomous. But has not such a person clearly forfeited autonomy? Must autonomy involve a particular content, a substantive and not merely procedural independence from others?

I shall argue that the conception of autonomy that insists upon substantive independence is not one that has a claim to our respect as an ideal. It is a conception which violates one of the constraints I imposed in Chapter 1 – that of being consistent with other important values we hold. In particular it makes autonomy inconsistent with loyalty, objectivity, commitment, benevolence, and love.

21

II

Let me begin with examples of philosophers who view substantive independence as an essential part of autonomy.

The autonomous man . . . may do what another tells him, but not because he has been told to do it. . . . By accepting as final the commands of the others, he forfeits his autonomy . . . a promise to abide by the will of the majority creates an obligation, but it does so precisely by giving up one's autonomy.[1]

An autonomous agent must be independent-minded. He must not have to depend on others for being told what he is to think or do . . . a person is "autonomous" to the degree that what he thinks and does cannot be explained without reference to his own activity of mind.[2]

[T]o be a moral agent is to be an autonomous or self-directed agent. . . . On this view, to deliver oneself over to a moral authority for directions about what to do is simply incompatible with being a moral agent. . . . [There is] a conflict between the role of worshipper, which by its very nature commits one to total subservience to God, and the role of moral agent, which necessarily involves autonomous decision making.[3]

What is essential to the person's remaining autonomous is that in any given case his mere recognition that a certain action is required by law does not settle the question of whether he will do it.[4]

In each of these cases what autonomy demands is that a person not defer independent judgment. Whether it be the legal system, or moral authority, or God that is in question, autonomy, on this view, requires the agent to retain control over his decisions and actions. In this view, promising, worship, obedience to command, conformity to law are all seen as inconsistent with autonomy.

We seem to be faced with a dilemma. On the one hand, this person is not thinking or deciding for himself in accordance with his preferences, tastes, and beliefs. He either does not form independent judgments about what he should do, or, if he does, they do not determine his actions. To predict his actions, we must know what his mother or his priest thinks he should do. How can he be autonomous?

1 Robert Paul Wolff, *In Defense of Anarchism* (New York: Harper & Row, 1970), 14, 41.
2 R. S. Downie, Elizabeth Telfer, "Autonomy," *Philosophy* 46 (1971), 301.
3 James Rachels, "God and Human Attitudes," *Religious Studies* 7 (1971), 334.
4 Thomas Scanlon, "A Theory of Freedom of Expression," *Philosophy and Public Affairs* 1 (Winter 1972), 215.

On the other hand, knowing what his mother wants is not sufficient to predict his actions either. We must make reference to his intentions to do what his mother wants. It is his decision, arrived at freely, backed by reasons, that makes his mother's wishes effective in determining his actions. He is doing what he wants to do. He is leading just the kind of life he thinks is worth leading. How can he not be autonomous?

The same issue arises in many contexts. Consider, for example, the use of sanctions in a legal system. Given the presence of such sanctions, it follows that the citizens have their freedom restricted. Have they also had their autonomy limited? If the idea of consent, in some form, to the rule of law makes sense, if we can legitimately think of the sanctions as being self-imposed, then it does not seem to me that their autonomy has been impaired.

Consider the selfish person and the generous one. There is something to the idea that the former may be sometimes freer than the latter insofar as he does not accept the needs of others as being reasons for altering his own plans and projects. Someone who cares for others must recognize that he is less free than those who are callous. But is the selfish person more autonomous than the benevolent one? If autonomy is thought of as substantive independence, he is. Must it be so thought of?

I want to argue that the conception of autonomy which insists upon substantive independence violates one of the initial constraints in that it makes autonomy inconsistent with other important values. Two examples should sufficiently illustrate the line of reasoning. Consider the nature of commitment. To be committed to a friend or cause is to accept the fact that one's actions, and even desires, are to some extent determined by the desires and needs of others. Even one's beliefs may be to some extent affected as in the case of a wife who refuses to believe her husband has done something evil, though the evidence seems to point clearly in that direction. To be devoted to a cause is to be governed by what needs to be done, or by what the group decides. It is no longer to be self-sufficient.

Consider, as another example, the case of loyalty. Royce defines this notion as follows: "The willing and practical and thoroughgoing devotion of a person to a cause."[5] He characterizes it phenomenologically in the following way:

5 Josiah Royce, *The Philosophy of Loyalty* (New York: Macmillan, 1908), 21.

23

The loyal man's cause is his cause by virtue of his assent . . . the devotion of the loyal man involves a sort of restraint or submission of his natural desires to his cause . . . the loyal man serves. That is, he does not merely follow his own impulses. He looks to his cause for guidance. This tells him what to do, and he does it.[5]

This emphasis on the external and its command of the will is exactly right. But Royce goes on to point out precisely those features that allow the loyal man to remain, at least on my account, autonomous: "His devotion is his own. He chooses, it, or, at all events, approves it."[5]

A similar difficulty faces the conception of autonomy that requires substantive independence when it deals with standards of excellence, with tradition and authority, and even logical necessity. All will be in conflict with autonomy.

It has been suggested that this form of argument proves too much. For there are other ideals, such as liberty, which also conflict with values like loyalty, love, promising, and other forms of commitment. Yet we do not deny that liberty is valuable. Nor do we search for a weaker conception of liberty that will avoid such conflicts.

I do not think this objection is sound, but the argument against it requires making a number of distinctions. The view goes like this: If I promise to meet you tomorrow, then I am no longer free to do something else. The whole point of promising is to commit oneself to a particular course of action, thus narrowing one's options from the larger selection that existed prior to the act of promising. One is no longer "at liberty" to be out of town or to spend one's time in other ways.

But these limitations on one's freedom of action are not the kinds of limitation that are associated with attacks on the ideal of political liberty. They are not the imposition of another's wishes upon one's own by the use of force. They do not limit one's options externally by attaching a sanction to options which did not have that price attached to them prior to the intervention of another agent. But these features are what we are objecting to when we assert that, say, there is a presumption in favor of liberty, that is if another agent proposes to limit our options in such fashion, he must give a justification of his actions.

Political liberty may be inconsistent (contingently) with other values we hold. For example, being free to use one's talents to make

24

as much money as one can may be incompatible with a certain degree of equality in a society. But it is a contingent fact that the exercise of this liberty may diminish equality. It is not that liberty itself conflicts with equality. The conflict of autonomy, considered as a substantive notion, with other values is not contingent but necessary. There is no possible world in which one could remain both substantively independent and commit oneself to a cause or a person. Robert P. Wolff is surely correct that one cannot be both autonomous in his sense and be under an obligation to obey the law simply because it is the law.[6]

There is, however, something correct about the belief that obligation is inconsistent with one idea of being free. When I bind myself or find myself in a situation in which my options are limited by the existence of the needs of others, I do feel (or, at least it is possible that I might feel) a sense of restraint. After all, one does give up something when one has children or enters certain personal relationships. The freedom that is lost is being able to do whatever is in one's immediate self-interest, or what is most pleasurable or convenient. I might prefer to read a novel than visit an aged relative, and the demands of the situation constrain my will. But this sense of freedom is not considered to be one that ought always to be honored, precisely because it manifests the kinds of conflicts with other values we have mentioned.

III

I want now to argue that the conception of autonomy that involves substantive independence leads to theoretical mistakes about political and moral authority. By relying on a weaker conception of autonomy, we can still argue for and provide reasons for the normative claims about authority we want to make. In short, we don't need it and it's not a very good thing anyway.

Consider Wolff's use of the strong conception of autonomy to deny the legitimacy of any state. Part of the problem with his argument undoubtedly stems from an overly strict idea of what authority consists of. If authority is supposed to mean obeying

6 Wolff *defines* autonomy so that "the autonomous man, insofar as he is autonomous, is not subject to the will of another." Wolff, *In Defense of Anarchism*, p. 14.

25

commands just because they are commands, then nobody has ever argued for the legitimacy (even the intelligibility) of that idea of authority. There are always some assumptions being made about the nature of the state that is issuing the commands, or the ways in which the state is formed and functions. But even on more reasonable views of authority (these which somehow ground it in knowledge or utility or consent), it will turn out that authority is inconsistent with autonomy. For even explicit agreement to obey is viewed as forfeiture of substantive independence, and therefore, autonomy. Now I agree that promises or commitments do involve forfeiture of substantive independence. The point of a promise is to renounce (at least within some limits) the right to think about what I should do. If I promise to return your book tomorrow, then it is no longer open for me to reflect as to what disposition I should make of the book. If I commit my time or my talents or my funds to a cause, then by doing so I foreclose the possibility of allocating these in other ways. But why view these as forfeitures of autonomy?

Well, what difference does it make? Call it what you will. Isn't this a mere quibble about words? No. For it is only because Wolff believes, with Kant, that autonomy is the "primary obligation of man" that he claims that *because* authority is inconsistent with autonomy, there can be no (legitimate) authority. I am claiming that if autonomy, as Wolff conceives it, is inconsistent with promising and commitment, it has no claim to be the supreme value.

What is valuable about autonomy is that the commitments and promises a person makes be ones he views as his, as part of the person he wants to be, so that he defines himself via those commitments. But whether they be long-term or short, prima facie or absolute, permanent or temporary, is not what contributes to their value. Though, indeed, there may be good reasons for limiting one's abandonment of substantive independence.

Scanlon's views seem to oscillate between a weaker conception of autonomy and a stronger one, but there are ambiguities of expression in his presentation that make it unclear to me exactly what his position is. He starts out with what he calls an "extremely weak" notion of autonomy:

An autonomous person cannot accept without independent consideration the judgment of others as to what he should do or believe. He may rely on the judgment of others, but when he does so he must be prepared to advance independent reasons for thinking their judgment likely to be correct, and to weigh the evidential value of their opinion against contrary evidence.[7]

Note here the ambiguity of the idea of there being independent reasons for thinking someone's judgment likely to be correct. These could be reasons for thinking his *judgment* likely to be correct, that is, for believing the content of his judgment correct. Or they could be reasons for thinking *his* judgment to be correct, that is, for thinking *him* likely to be right. These correspond to a stronger and weaker notion of autonomy. Let us assume that Scanlon is to be read in the weaker sense. We needn't be prepared to give independent reasons for the judgment but only for relying on the authority.

This is inconsistent with what he says later about what kinds of actions count as a forfeiture of autonomy.

It is quite conceivable that a person who recognized in himself a fatal weakness for certain kinds of bad arguments might conclude that everyone would be better off if he were to rely entirely on the judgment of his friends in certain crucial matters. Acting on this conclusion, he might enter into an agreement subject to periodic review by him, empowering them to shield him from any source of information likely to divert him from their counsel on the matter in question. Such an agreement is not obviously irrational, nor, if entered into voluntarily, for a limited time, and on the basis of the person's own knowledge of himself and those he proposes to trust, does it appear to be inconsistent with his autonomy. The same would be true if the proposed trustees were in fact the authorities of the state.[7]

But then why does he think that autonomy is inconsistent with accepting a conclusive obligation to obey the law.

What is essential to the person's remaining autonomous is that in any given case his mere recognition that a certain action is required by law does not settle the question of whether he will do it.[8]

Could not a rule-utilitarian come to the conclusion that welfare would best be maximized by not having people make their own calculations about each law, but rather (at least within some range of issues) simply to obey laws that have been established by legitimate procedures? Is such a position necessarily a forfeiture of autonomy?

It may be that there are good reasons, as Scanlon suggests, for

7 Scanlon, "A Theory of Freedom," 217.
8 Scanlon, Ibid., 216.

citizens not to grant such authority to the state. But I do not think the argument can rely simply on what autonomous persons can do consistent with their autonomy. If a citizen had reasons for granting such powers, if that is the kind of state he thinks it is good to live in, and the kind of citizen he wants to be, then in my conception of autonomy he can remain autonomous while granting such authority.

It is not difficult to understand how the conception of autonomy that emphasizes substantive independence (it is *one* conception, so I am not claiming misuse of the concept) is connected with ideas of rugged individualism. It is more difficult to see why theorists like Wolff and Scanlon, who oppose such a tradition, make the error of using a similar conception of autonomy. One explanation is in terms of the connection with the notion of responsibility.

One of the main reasons for being unwilling to abandon substantive independence as an ingredient of the ideal of autonomy is the fear that the link with responsibility may be broken. And it is certainly true that the notion of autonomy has been linked with that of responsibility. But exactly what this link is, and on what features of autonomy it depends, is very obscure.

The simplest answer is clearly wrong. This is the view that only the autonomous person is, or can be held, responsible for what he does. The person who, in Mill's words, "lets the world, or his own portion of it, choose his life plan for him"[9] does not thereby escape responsibility. He does not do so if he lacks substantive independence for he cannot evade responsibility by doing what another tells him to do. He is responsible precisely for doing *that*. Nor can he escape responsibility by refusing to think about or reflect on the kind of person he is and should be. "I didn't think" is hardly an excuse. What may affect responsibility is interference with a person's autonomous action when the person is not in a position to realize this is occurring, or to do much about it if he does. If my will is overborne or undermined, then in suitable circumstances the responsibility for what I have done may shift to those who have interfered with my autonomy. But this link with responsibility is preserved by my account. It therefore cannot be used as part of an argument for substantive independence.

9 J. S. Mill, "On Liberty, " in *Utilitarianism and on Liberty*, ed. Mary Warnock (London: Fontana Library Edition, 1962), 186.

In my conception, the autonomous person can be a tyrant or a slave, a saint or sinner, a rugged individualist or champion of fraternity, a leader or follower. But I believe that there are contingent connections between being autonomous and the substantive nature of such a person's values. Although there are no a priori truths about the content of an autonomous person's values, one can speculate about psychological and sociological connections. It seems plausible that those who practice in their daily life a critical reflection on their own value structure will tend to be suspicious of modes of thought that rely on the uncritical acceptance of authority, tradition, and custom. They will be disposed to value the kind of substantive independence ranked so highly by philosophers like Mill and Humboldt. Of course, while these may be linked, one must not assume which is causally prior. It is as likely that one begins to develop autonomy as a result of becoming skeptical about the received wisdom as that one becomes skeptical about the "done" thing because one values autonomy.

Another speculation is that as people critically reflect on the procedural independence or lack of it in the ways in which they acquire their tastes and preferences, they will change those preferences that they discover are the result of manipulation or deception. One could try and develop a theory to distinguish between what have been referred to by radical critics as "real" versus "artificial" ("true" versus "false") needs and desires in this way. A real need is one such that the discovery of its genesis does not tend to undermine one's acceptance and identification with that need. Both of these conjectures, then, will lend strength to the view that there is some connection between autonomy and substantive independence.

IV

Having developed a conception of autonomy, and argued that alternative conceptions create problems in our understanding of their value, I want now to consider the issue of the value of autonomy as I conceive it. Why is the development, preservation, and enhancement of autonomy something to be desired? Why do contemporary political theorists like John Rawls, Thomas Scanlon, and Ronald Dworkin assign such a fundamental role to the idea of autonomy?

This question is made more difficult, in a way, by the particular conception I am defending. For autonomy, as substantive independence, at least provides a content that one can attempt to justify as worthy of admiration. The self-sufficient, independent, person relying on his own resources and intellect is a familiar hero presented in novels by Ayn Rand and westerns by John Ford. Whether or not one is attracted to that model, one can understand its hold on others. But a conception of autonomy that has no particular content, that emphasizes self-definition in abstraction from the self that is so defined, seems too thin, too formal to be of much value.

Nevertheless, I believe that this rather weak notion of autonomy plays a fundamental role in our conception of what it is to respect other persons and to accept the moral point of view.

Let me begin by considering at the most abstract level what is involved in moral reasoning. Every moral theory has some conception of treating others as equal in certain ways to oneself. For the utilitarian, this is represented by treating the interests of each alike in the calculation of utility. For the natural rights theorists, all persons are assumed to have equal rights. For the Kantian, I may only act in ways in which I am prepared to accept that all others act.

Corresponding to these notions of equality are conceptions of moral justification. For the utilitarian, it is to see that the action is justified from the point of view of an impartial observer considering what would maximize utility. For the rights theorist and the Kantian, a justification must be acceptable to each individual. Each individual has a veto over what may be done to him.

All these theories share the view that what we are allowed to do must reflect in some way the preferences of those who are affected by what we do. This reflection may be simple – the utilitarian's equal weighing of everybody's preferences. Or it may be more complex as in Rawls's contention that certain preferences may be ignored; roughly, those that aim at states of affairs that would violate the principles of justice. For various strong theories of natural rights, autonomy is preserved by requiring unanimous consent to restrictions of liberty.

Further, all these theories accept some idea of choice under conditions of procedural independence. These may be specified indirectly as with the utilitarian claim that each person is the best judge of his own interests. Or they may be built into the metatheory, as with Rawls's rejection of "threat-advantage," and the requirement of unanimity.

Underlying the various ideas of moral justification is a prohibition against treating people in such a way that they cannot share the purposes of those who are so treating them. This is brought out in Kant's theory in the idea of using people simply as a means to one's own ends. It underlies the emphasis on publicity in Rawls's theory.

Behind these common assumptions is a shared conception of what a person is. What makes an individual the particular person he is is his life-plan, his projects. In pursuing autonomy, one shapes one's life, one constructs its meaning. The autonomous person gives meaning to his life.

If this is right, then one sees a number of reasons why autonomy is a relatively weak and contentless notion. First, it must be so because people can give meaning to their lives in all kinds of ways: from stamp collecting to taking care of one's invalid parents. There is no particular way of giving shape and meaning to a life. Second, any feature that is going to be fundamental in moral thinking must be a feature that persons share. But any substantive conception of autonomy is not likely to be shared. Morality is what is owed to everyone. More intimate relationships such as friend or lover must respond to particular qualities, to lives shaped in particular ways. Moral respect is owed to all because all have the capacity for defining themselves.

It may be objected that whereas all persons, at least those of normal intelligence and rationality, have the capacity to reflect upon their lives and shape them, it is not the case that all persons have an equal capacity. After all, like any other capacity – say the capacity to identify empathetically with others or the capacity to postpone current satisfaction for future gain – it is a product of one's biological characteristics and one's environmental circumstances. It is extremely improbable, although I suppose logically possible, that each person's capacity should be of the same strength and power as all other persons. This is a similar problem concerning rationality for those who seek to ground moral respect in that capacity.

I believe the right response is that this is a case of a capacity which has a significant threshold. Our conception of a person is of a creature who possesses this capacity above some particular level.

31

That some persons will be very much above the level is not important, morally speaking, although it may be significant for some purposes.

On the view defended here autonomy is a capacity that is (partly) constitutive of what it is to be an agent. It is a capacity that we have a responsibility to exercise and that grounds our notion of having a *character*. As Butler puts it: "We are agents. Our constitution is put in our own power. We are charged with it, and therefore are accountable for any disorder or violation of it."[10]

There are various connections between autonomy as I have conceived it and metaphysical and attitudinal features of persons. Our notion of who we are, of self-identity, of being *this* person is linked to our capacity to find and re-fine oneself. The exercise of the capacity is what makes a life *mine*. And, if I am to recognize others as persons, as independent centers of consciousness, as *them*, then there is a requirement that I give weight to the way they define and value the world in deciding how I should act.

There is an intellectual error that threatens to arise whenever autonomy has been defended as crucial or fundamental: This is that the notion is elevated to a higher status than it deserves. Autonomy *is* important, but so is the capacity for sympathetic identification with others, or the capacity to reason prudentially, or the virtue of integrity. Similarly, although it is important to respect the autonomy of others, it is also important to respect their welfare, or their liberty, or their rationality. Theories that base everything on any single aspect of human personality, on any one of a number of values, always tend toward the intellectually imperialistic. One way in which this is done is by assimilating other concepts to that of autonomy. I have tried to avoid this by sharply distinguishing autonomy from other concepts. But having done this there is the tendency to claim that the concept is not only distinct but also supreme. I believe that autonomy is both important normatively and fundamental conceptually. Neither of these precludes the possibility that other concepts are both important and fundamental.

I have put forward a certain ideal of the person and given reasons why such a conception is deeply rooted in our existing conceptual scheme, and why this conception is to be valued. There are competing conceptions and the choice between them may at some level

10 Joseph Butler, *Five Sermons*, ed. S. Darwall (Indianapolis: Hackett, 1983), 15.

not be capable of rational discussion. But, at this point in the history of moral philosophy, we are far from that point. As with other fundamental moral concepts, its appraisal depends upon working out the long and complex strands by which the concept is tied to other parts of our moral and scientific theory, which problems are resolved, clarified, dissolved. And, of course, what the costs of accepting the theory are. The following essays represent such an exploration – in theory and practice.

3

Moral autonomy

The will is therefore not merely subject to the law, but is so subject that it must be considered as also making the law for itself and precisely on this account as first of all subject to the law (of which it can regard itself as the author).

Kant, *The Metaphysics of Morals*

[Virtue] is not a troubling oneself about a particular and isolated morality of one's own . . . the striving for a positive morality of one's own is futile, and in its very nature impossible of attainment . . . to be moral is to live in accordance with the moral tradition of one's own country.

Hegel, *The Phenomenology of Spirit*

1. There is a philosophical view about morality that is shared by moral philosophers as divergent as Kant, Kierkegaard, Nietzsche, Royce, Hare, Popper, Sartre, and Wolff. It is a view of the moral agent as necessarily autonomous. It is this view that I wish to understand and evaluate in this essay. I speak of a view and not a thesis because the position involves not merely a conception of autonomy but connected views about the nature of moral principles, of moral epistemology, of rationality, and of responsibility.

2. I shall begin by distinguishing a number of ways of explicating the notion of moral autonomy. In the philosophical debate very different notions have been confused, and because they are involved in claims that range from the trivially true to the profoundly false it is essential to distinguish them.

3. The most general formulation of moral autonomy is: A person is morally autonomous if and only if his moral principles are his own. The following are more specific characterizations of what it might mean for moral principles to be one's own.

This chapter was originally published in *Morals, Science and Sociality*, eds. T. Engelhardt and D. Callahan (Hastings-on-Hudson, N.Y.: The Hastings Center, 1978), 56–70. Reprinted by permission.

1. A person is morally autonomous if and only if he is the author of his moral principles, their originator.
2. A person is morally autonomous if and only if he chooses his moral principles.
3. A person is morally autonomous if and only if the ultimate authority or source of his moral principles is his will.
4. A person is morally autonomous if and only if he decides which moral principles to accept as binding upon him.
5. A person is morally autonomous if and only if he bears the responsibility for the moral theory he accepts and the principles he applies.
6. A person is morally autonomous if and only if he refuses to accept others as moral authorities, that is, he does not accept without independent consideration the judgment of others as to what is morally correct.

4. In this essay I am not concerned with other issues that have been discussed under the heading of autonomy. I am not concerned with the general question of what it is for an individual to act autonomously. I am not concerned with various views that have been discussed under the heading of the autonomy of morals – whether one can derive an "ought" from an "is"; or the relations, if any, between facts and values; or whether the acceptance of moral principles necessarily carries with it a motivating influence upon conduct. Clearly, there are connections between one's views on these matters and the issue of moral autonomy. I do not propose to draw them here.

5. What could it mean to say that a person's moral principles are his own? We have already identified them as "his" when we referred to them as "a person's moral principles." But how do we make that identification? In terms of considerations such as the following: Which moral principles occur as part of the best explanation of a person's actions? Which moral principles would the person defend as correct? Which moral principles does he use as a basis for self-criticism? For the criticism of others? Which moral principles make his enthymematic moral arguments into valid arguments? There are practical problems in making this identification – the issue of rationalization, and theoretical problems (*akrasia* – are they the person's principles if he doesn't act in accordance with them?), but there is no special problem connected with autonomy. That issue concerns the notion of moral principles being his "own."

6. How could a person's moral principles not be his own? Not by being at the same time someone else's. For the fact that we share a common set of principles no more shows them not to be my

own than our sharing a taste for chocolate shows that my taste is not my own. Perhaps I borrowed your principles, or illegitimately appropriated them, or simply found them and never bothered to acknowledge their true owner. But all of these notions (as with the idea on which they trade – property) assume the notion that is to be explained. They all assume that somebody's principles are his own and that somebody else is not in the appropriate relation to his principles that the first person is.

7. With property, how one acquired it is essential. Perhaps that is what we must look for here as well. One suggestion is that we create or invent our moral principles. Sartre speaks of a young man deciding between joining the Free French or staying with his aged mother as being "obliged to invent the law for himself." Kant says the will "must be considered as also making the law for itself."

8. If this is what moral autonomy demands, then it is impossible on both empirical and conceptual grounds. On empirical grounds this view denies our *history*. We are born in a given environment with a given set of biological endowments. We mature more slowly than other animals and are deeply influenced by parents, siblings, peers, culture, class, climate, schools, accident, genes, and the accumulated history of the species. It makes no more sense to suppose we invent the moral law for ourselves than to suppose that we invent the language we speak for ourselves.

9. This is perhaps – I doubt it – a contingent difficulty. There are logical difficulties as well. For suppose one did invent a set of principles independently of the various influences enumerated above. What would make them *moral* principles? I may act in accordance with them and take my deviation from them as a defect but that is not enough. I might be engaged in some kind of private ritual.

10. A central feature of moral principles is their social character. By this I mean, partly, that their interpretation often bears a conventional character. What my duties are as a parent, how close a relative must be to be owed respect, what duties of aid are owed to another, how one expresses regret or respect, are to some extent relative to the understandings of a given society. In addition, moral rules often function to provide solutions to a coordination problem – a situation in which what one agent chooses to do depends upon his expectations of what other agents will do – agents whose choices are in turn dependent on what the first agent will do. Such con-

ventions depend upon the mutual convergence of patterns of behavior. The principles of morality are also social in that they have what H. L. A. Hart calls an internal aspect. They provide common standards that are used as the basis of criticism and demands for obedience. All of these preclude individual invention.

11. Does this imply that moral reform is impossible? Not at all. It just implies that moral reform takes place against a background of accepted understandings about our moral relationships with one another. And *these* are not invented. Moral reforms (almost?) always take the form of attacking inconsistencies in the accepted moral framework, refusals to extend rights and privileges that are seen as legitimate already. Analogy and precedent – the weapons of the conservatives – are the engines of reform as well.

12. If I do not and cannot make the moral law for myself, at least, so it is claimed, I can always choose to accept or reject the existing moral framework. It is up to me to decide what is morally proper. This is the proper interpretation of Sartre's claim that his young man is "obliged to invent the law for himself." Nothing in the situation he faces shows him what to do. The competing claims are equally compelling. He must simply decide.

13. Choice and decision do enter here but it is crucial to see how late in the game they enter. For Sartre (and the young man) already know they are faced with competing claims, and that these claims are of comparable moral force. That a son has obligations to his aged mother; that a citizen has a duty to defend his country against evil men; that neither of these claims is obviously more important or weighty than the other – none of these are matters of choice or decision. Indeed, the idea that they are is incompatible with the quality of tragic choice or moral dilemma that the situation poses. For if one could just choose the moral quality of one's situation, then all the young man would have to do is choose to regard his mother's welfare as morally insignificant, or choose to regard the Nazi invasion as a good thing, or choose to regard one of these evils as much more serious than the other.

14. Could someone *choose* to regard accidental injuries as having the same moral gravity as intentional ones? Utilitarians, some of whom say something like this, do so on the basis of a *theory*.

15. Still, if one cannot originate one's moral principles, and if the relevance of various factors to moral decision making is not always a matter of choice, the ultimate weighting of the moral

factors is the agent's decision and his alone. A moral agent must retain autonomy, must make his own moral choices. The problem is to give this idea content in such a way that it escapes being trivial (who else could make my decisions?) or false (the denial of authority, tradition, and community).

16. How could a person's moral principles not be his own? Here is one case. It is from *Anna Karenina*.

Stefan Arkadyevitch always read a liberal paper. It was not extreme in its views, but advocated those principles held by the majority of people. In spite of the fact that he was not really interested in science, or art, or politics, he strongly adhered to the same views on all such subjects as the majority and this paper in particular advocated, and changed them only when the majority changed. Or rather, it might be said, he did not change them at all – they changed themselves imperceptibly.

Here the beliefs are not his because they are borrowed; and they are borrowed without even being aware of their source; and, it is implied, Stefan is not capable of giving some account of their validity – not even an account which, say, stresses the likelihood of the majority being correct, or the necessity for moral consensus. All of these are important here – not just the borrowing.

17. It is not sufficient for showing that my moral beliefs are not my own to show that my holding them has been causally influenced by others. Almost all our beliefs have been so influenced. Nor is it enough to show that although I have reasons that justify my beliefs, those reasons are not the causes of my beliefs. I may have acquired a belief from my father in, say, the importance of equality. But if I now have reasons that justify my belief, it is my belief. Nor is it enough to show that among the reasons I present to justify my belief are reasons that make reference to the beliefs of others.

18. If I believe Father knows best, and I do what Father tells me to do because I believe Father knows best, then Father's principles become mine as well. To deny this is to assume that what is mine must only be mine.

19. Underlying the notions of autonomy considered so far are assumptions about objectivity, the role of conscientiousness, obligation, responsibility, and the way in which we come to see that certain moral claims are correct. I shall argue that with respect to all of these issues the doctrine of autonomy in any of the interpretations (1–4) is one-sided and misleading.

20. These doctrines of autonomy conflict with views we hold

about objectivity in morals. We believe that the answering of moral questions is a rational process not just in the sense that there are better and worse ways of going about it, but that it matters what answer we find. It makes sense to speak of someone as being mistaken or misled in his moral views. The idea of objectivity is tied up with that which is independent of will or choice. That a certain inference is valid, that a certain event causes another, that a certain course of conduct is illegal, that Bach is superior to Bachrach, that Gandhi was a better person than Hitler, that the manufacturer who substituted an inert substance for the active ingredient in Ipecac did an evil thing, are independent of my will or decision.

21. There is a paradox for notions of autonomy that rely on the agent's will or decision. Consider the statement that moral agents ought to be autonomous. Either that statement is an objectively true statement or it is not. If it is, then there is at least one moral assertion whose claim to validity does not rest on its being accepted by a moral agent. If it is not, then no criticism can be made of a moral agent who refuses to accept it.

22. Another form of the paradox. Consider the following two claims.

1. P ought to be autonomous
2. P chooses not to be autonomous

Does P have any reason to accept (1)?

23. We can see in Kant the confusion engendered by his attempt to reconcile objectivity and autonomy. For Kant the moral law does *not* obtain its objective character by being chosen or willed by us. The categorical imperative commands us to act on that maxim which we *can* will as universal law. In a second formulation we are enjoined to act *as if* the maxim of our action were to become through our will a universal law of nature. What is essential is that one could will to act in such and such a way, not that we actually so will.

24. But when Kant faces the problem of how such an imperative can be binding on us he reverts to the notion of willing. The argument is that a categorical imperative cannot be binding because of some interest I have – because then it would be hypothetical. So, in the philosophical move that Hilary Putnam calls the "what else argument," Kant concludes that it must be binding because we have legislated it ourselves. But there are other possibilities, in-

cluding the thesis that there are objective requirements of reason which provide their own form of rational motivation.

25. For John Rawls, the objectivity of principles is defined in terms of their being the principles that would be chosen by free, equal, and rational beings. As such they are binding upon individuals whether or not they view them as binding. But agents are able to put themselves in the position of being choosers, to follow the arguments for the principles, and to desire that everyone (including themselves) accept such principles as binding. To the extent that they are motivated in this manner – and not, say, by mere submission to parental authority – they are morally autonomous.[1]

26. In addition, there arises at the level of the interpretation and application of moral principles a substantive political conception of autonomy. Given the fact that real persons, even if they accepted a common moral framework, will have different and conflicting ideas of the correct interpretation of that theory, a state may be required to recognize political autonomy of its citizens. That is, it may not restrict the liberty of individuals unless it can justify such restrictions with arguments that the person himself can (given certain minimal rationality) see as correct. Such a doctrine can be invoked in defense of freedom of expression and conscience. But it is important to note that this argument applies to a specific area of moral life – the limits of state power. And even there, I have argued elsewhere, there are difficulties.[2]

27. Preoccupation with autonomy carries with it the attribution of supremacy to the concepts of integrity and conscientiousness. For if what is morally correct is what one has decided for oneself is correct, then for another to interfere with one's freedom of action based on that decision is to stifle moral personality and encourage hypocrisy. Politically this leads to the type of philosophical anarchism that Robert Paul Wolff espouses.[3] Socially it leads to the rejection of any use of community and peer pressure to limit the liberty of individuals. This is often defended in the name of Mill – a defense that only charity could attribute to a misreading (as it

1 John Rawls, *A Theory of Justice* (Cambridge: Harvard University Press, 1971), 516–19.
2 Gerald Dworkin, "Non–neutral Principles," *Journal of Philosophy* 71 (August 15, 1974).
3 Robert Paul Wolff, *In Defense of Anarchism* (New York: Harper & Row, 1970).

is obvious that anyone who believes this cannot have read Mill at all).

28. At the very least a defender of autonomy must distinguish between autonomy of judgment and autonomy of action. The arguments in favor of allowing people to determine for themselves what is right are more compelling than those that favor allowing people always to act in accordance with their beliefs. It is one thing to argue in defense of freedom of expression from premises concerning what individuals who wish to retain autonomy would be willing to grant the state by way of authority to limit expression. It is quite another to argue, as Wolff does, that law qua law creates no obligation to obey.

29. As for integrity – that second-order value which consists in acting in accordance with one's first-order values – it is not to be despised. There is something admirable about the person who acts on principle, even if his principles are awful. But there is also something to be said for Huck Finn, who "knowing" that slavery was right, and believing that he was morally damned if he helped Jim to escape, was willing to sacrifice his integrity in favor of his humanitarian impulses.

30. A moral theory that stresses the supremacy of autonomy will have difficulties with the concept of obligation. As the etymology suggests, to be obliged is to be bound. And to be bound is to have one's will restricted; to have one's moral status altered so that it is no longer one's choice how one should act. The usual suggestion of the defender of autonomy is that one can, so to speak, tie oneself up. And this is the only way one becomes bound. All obligation is ultimately self-imposed, hence a product of one's decision or choice to be so limited.

I am persuaded that moral obligations, strictly so-called, arise from freely chosen contractual commitments between or among rational agents who have entered into some continuing and organized interaction with one another.[4]

(How the notions of autonomy, individualism, Protestantism, and contract emerge [and merge] in moral, social, religious, and economic thought is a subject [still] worth historical investigation.)

4 Robert Paul Wolff, *The Autonomy of Reason* (New York: Harper & Row, 1973), 219.

31. This attempted solution cannot succeed. Tying oneself up is binding only if the knot is no longer in one's hands. For if I can, at will, release myself I am only in appearance bound. As Hume put it with respect to the obligations created by promises, on this view the will "has no object to which it could tend but must return to itself *in infinitum.*"[5] To say that promises create obligations because they create expectations is true enough but of no help here. For that these expectations have moral weight is not itself chosen or decided by the maker of the promise.

32. Another way of looking at this. From the temporal perspective the commitments of my earlier self must bind (to some degree) my later self. It cannot always be open for the later self to renounce the commitments of the earlier self. This implies that even self-imposed obligations create a world of "otherness" – a world that is independent of my (current) will and that is not subject to my choices and decisions. The distance between my earlier and later selves is only quantitatively different from that between myself and others.

33. In his discussion of the one state he believes has authority and is consistent with autonomy – unanimous direct democracy – Wolff fails to see this point. He argues that there is no sacrifice of autonomy because all laws are accepted by every citizen. But this is only true at a given point in time. What if the individual changes his mind about the wisdom or goodness of the law? Is he then bound to obey it?

34. Leaving the internal difficulties to the side, the claim that all obligations are self-imposed does not fit the moral facts. That I have obligations of gratitude to my aged parents, of aid to the stranger attacked by thieves, of obedience to the laws of a democratic and just state, of rectification to those treated unjustly by my ancestors or nation are matters that are independent of my voluntary commitments.

35. The defender of autonomy has a particular picture of the role of discovery in morality.

[The moral agent] may learn from others about his moral obligations, but only in the sense that a mathematician learns from other mathematicians – namely by hearing from them arguments whose validity he recognizes

---

5 David Hume, *Treatise of Human Nature* (Oxford: Clarendon Press, 1888), 517–18.

even though he did not think of them himself. He does not learn in the sense that one learns from an explorer, by accepting as true his accounts of things one cannot see for oneself.[6]

This picture is inaccurate even for the mathematician. Mathematicians often accept results on the word of other mathematicians without going through the proofs for themselves. And they may do so (particularly) in fields in which they do not possess the techniques to assess the proof even if they were inclined to do so.

36. The image of the explorer is an interesting one and is analogous to the role of the seer in the moral systems of various tribal peoples. Lest one think that this view is one that only "primitives" hold, compare the role of the "practically wise" man in Aristotle.

37. For Aristotle moral virtue is a disposition to choose that is developed in the process of choosing. We do not do good acts because we are already good (at first anyway). We do good acts, and in doing so become good. This is paradoxical. How are we to identify those acts which are good, if we are not ourselves already good? By aiming at the mean which is determined by the "proper rule." How do we identify the proper rule? It is "the rule by which a practically wise man would determine it." Thus, to be morally virtuous one must follow the example or precept of one who is practically wise.

38. Such an account, which places reliance on the exemplary individual, on imitation of goodness, on what would in a more barbarous term be called role-modeling, seems to me to be, if not the whole story, at least a significant part of it. Such a view has its own vices of excess. There is, no doubt, the morally unappetizing sight of the person who abandons all attempts to think critically about who he is imitating, who imitates out of laziness or fear or sycophancy. This excess has received its share of attention from an excessively protestant and individualistic age. I am calling attention to the opposite defect. The refusal to acknowledge the very idea of moral authority, the equation of imitation with animal characteristics (copycat; monkey see, monkey do), the identification of maturity with doing things without help, by (and for?) oneself.

39. Consider the fifth interpretation of autonomy – being responsible for the moral theory we believe correct and for the interpretation of the principles that follow from it. Leaving aside general

6 Wolff, *In Defense of Anarchism*, 7.

metaphysical doubts about freedom of the will and empirical doubts about causes of our conduct which are beyond our control, this thesis seems to me correct but vacuous. One cannot evade responsibility by asserting that one was only following orders or doing what everybody does or accepting the general will. But this leaves completely open the issue of whether one ought to be autonomous in the sense of (6), that is, being prepared to examine one's principles in a critical fashion. Whether one does so or not, one will still be (held) responsible.

It is the confusion of these two distinct notions that leads Aiken to assert that "no man is morally responsible for actions unless they are performed for the sake of principles which he cannot in conscience disavow."[7]

This implies that all one has to do to avoid responsibility is either be completely unprincipled or accept principles without conscientious scrutiny.

40. We come now to the last interpretation of autonomy. A person is morally autonomous only if he

cannot accept without independent consideration the judgment of others as to what he should do. If he relies on the judgment of others he must be prepared to advance independent reasons for thinking their judgment likely to be correct.[8]

41. This is the denial of any strong notion of moral authority. On this view none of the following justifications could be acceptable.

• These principles are acceptable because they are the revealed word of God.
• These principles are acceptable because they are part of the moral tradition to which I belong.
• These principles are acceptable because the elders have pronounced them acceptable.
• These principles are acceptable because they are those of my class or my clan or my comrades.
• These principles are acceptable because they are embodied in the common law or the Constitution.

7 Henry Aiken, *Reason and Conduct* (New York: Knopf, 1962), 143.
8 Thomas Scanlon, "A Theory of Freedom of Expression," *Philosophy and Public Affairs* I (Winter 1972), 216. This is not put forward by Scanlon as a notion of *moral* autonomy. I adopt his words for my own purposes.

- These principles are acceptable because they were passed on to me as part of my training as doctor, lawyer, Indian chief.
- These principles are acceptable because they are customary, or the ways of my father and my father's father.
- These principles are acceptable because they are in accord with Nature or the Tao or the course of evolution.
- These principles are acceptable because they are those of Gandhi or Thoreau or Socrates or Confucius or Jesus or Tolstoy.

42. The idea of there being independent reasons for thinking the judgments of an authority correct is ambiguous. There are reasons for thinking his *judgment* likely to be correct, that is, independent reasons for believing the content of his judgment correct. Or there can be independent reasons for thinking *his* judgment to be correct, that is, for thinking *him* likely to be right. Corresponding to these we have a weaker and stronger notion of "checking" an authority. In one case, having checked out his authority, we no longer check his advice in the particular case (weak checking). In the other case we may take his opinion into account but still seek independent verification (strong checking).

43. It will be useful to turn for a moment to the idea of epistemological authority. Do we not frequently accept without independent consideration the judgment of others as to what we should believe or do in nonmoral matters? If I am uncertain about a statistical question, or what that pain in my leg is, or whether this appliance should be purchased, or why the thermostat is not working, or whether Aristotle believed there was a mind–body problem, or why the soufflé keeps falling, or the number of words for "snow" that the Eskimo have, I consult an authority. I take his advice, I rely on his judgment, I accept what he says. I do not – unless there are special reasons for doubt – investigate the matter independently to see if he is correct.

44. There are various reasons why such a policy is rational. We lack time, knowledge, training, skill. In addition there is a necessary and useful division of labor. It is more efficient for each of us to specialize in a few areas of competence and be able to draw, when we need it, upon the resources and expertise of others. Knowledge is socially stored and there are evolutionary advantages for a species that does not require each individual member to acquire and retain all the knowledge needed for survival and reproduction. It may also be true that our reliance upon authority assumes that some-

45

where in the chain of authority conferral, someone has engaged in (weak or strong) checking. But that each individual do so, on every occasion, is neither necessary nor rational.

45. It is said that things are different with morality.

In the domain of science and logic . . . situations often arise in which we properly defer to the authority of observers whom we recognize to be more competent or qualified than ourselves. And it is because of that, without qualms, we accept certain statements as objectively true even though we ourselves do not fully see why they are so. But in morals such situations can hardly arise . . . no one can be expected to conform his judgment and his will to certain allegedly objective principles which he has not in conscience made absolutely his own. Nor is this situation altered by the fact that some men take their principles from some "authority." For that authority can make no moral claims upon anyone who does not adopt it as *his* authority.[9]

46. There is no argument here, only assertion. But consider the following bad argument for the same claim by Hare.

It might be objected that moral questions are not peculiar in this respect – that we are free also to form our own opinions about such matters as whether the world is round . . . but we are free to form our own moral opinions in a much stronger sense than this. For if we say that the world is flat, we can in principle be shown certain facts such that, once we have admitted them, we cannot go on saying that the world is flat without being guilty of self-contradiction or misuse of language . . . nothing of the sort can be done in morals.[10]

This is mistaken on both counts. There are no facts – which are not logically equivalent to the roundness of the earth – which preclude a person from insisting upon an alternative explanation of them. Upholders of ad hoc and silly hypotheses are guilty neither of contradiction nor misuse of language. But if one wants to say this kind of thing, then one can say it in moral matters. To admit that I ran over your child's dog deliberately, without excuse, because I dislike both the dog and your child, and to go on saying that what I did was right, is as plausibly being guilty of self-contradiction or misuse of language.

47. We have not yet discovered an argument for the view that autonomy understood as critical, self-conscious reflection on one's moral principles plays a more distinctive or greater role in moral

9 Aiken, *Reason and Conduct*, 143.
10 R. M. Hare, *Freedom and Reason* (Oxford: Clarendon Press, 1963), 2.

reasoning than it does elsewhere in our theoretical or practical reasoning, for example, in scientific theorizing. Still, this conception of autonomy as critical reflection avoids the difficulties of the earlier interpretations. It is consistent with objectivity, for critical reflection is aimed at what is correct. It need not reject the view that some of us may be better at moral reasoning than others. It is compatible with the recognition of a notion of (limited) authority, and can accept the relevance (if not the conclusiveness) of tradition in moral life.

48. It is one ideal of morality, and like other ideals it may turn imperialistic and try to exclude alternative conceptions. But, as Michael Oakeshott observes, "[T]his is a corruption which every disposition recognized as a virtue is apt to suffer at the hands of fanatics."[11]

49. I have argued that there is no interesting thesis about moral autonomy which follows from any conceptual thesis about the nature of morality or moral agency. It is a substantive thesis and represents a particular conception of morality – one that, among other features, places a heavy emphasis on rules and principles rather than virtues and practices. Considered purely internally there are conceptual, moral, and empirical difficulties in defining and elaborating a conception of autonomy that is coherent and provides us with an ideal worthy of pursuit.

50. It is only through a more adequate understanding of notions such as tradition, authority, commitment, and loyalty, and of the forms of human community in which these have their roots, that we shall be able to develop a conception of autonomy free from paradox and worthy of admiration.

11 Michael Oakeshott, *On Human Conduct* (Oxford: Clarendon Press, 1975), 238.

4

Autonomy, science, and morality

The concept of autonomy has assumed increasing importance in contemporary moral theory. Appeals to the ideal of an autonomous moral agent play a role in grounding moral argument that appeals to sentiment or self-evidence or intuition played in earlier centuries. In such discussions moral judgments are often contrasted with factual or scientific judgments and claims are made about autonomy (as well as related notions such as authority and objectivity) in the moral context that are sharply distinguished from parallel claims in the scientific context. My aim in this essay is, as they say on prelims, to compare and contrast the nature of autonomy in morality and science.

In Chapter 1, I have characterized autonomy as the capacity of a person critically to reflect upon, and then attempt to accept or change, his or her preferences, desires, values, and ideals. The idea of moral autonomy is a particular case of this, and the rough idea is that persons are responsible for, and have the capacity for, determining for themselves the nature of the moral reasons, considerations, and principles on which they will act.

When I speak of autonomy I shall take this to be a property of persons and I shall only indirectly be concerned with the discussion that has proceeded under the heading of the autonomy of morality, that is, the connection or lack of connection between facts and values. I am primarily concerned with autonomy as specifying certain features of persons involved in their deliberations upon moral issues. I am concerned with moral autonomy and not the autonomy of morals.

As with the general notion of autonomy, there are a number of different and incompatible specifications of the root idea of self-determination in moral matters, as the idea of moral principles being "one's own" has various interpretations. The following are possible characterizations of what it might mean to be morally autonomous.

1. A person is morally autonomous if and only if she is the author of her moral principles, their originator.
2. A person is morally autonomous if and only if she chooses her moral principles.
3. A person is morally autonomous if and only if the ultimate authority or source of her moral principles is her will.
4. A person is morally autonomous if and only if she decides which moral principles to accept as binding upon her.
5. A person is morally autonomous if and only if she accepts moral responsibility for the principles she acts upon.
6. A person is morally autonomous if and only if she refuses to accept others as moral authorities.[1]

These are clearly not equivalent to one another. It is one thing, and surely false, to say that a person originates ab initio her moral framework; quite another to say that she finds herself confronted with one but bears the responsibility for accepting and acting in accordance with it. For certain purposes, for example, to combat certain extreme subjectivist doctrines, it would be important to explore the differences among these, but I am interested in formulating the doctrine in its most plausible versions and for this purpose the last three views are the ones of most interest.

Stated most broadly, the view is that in the moral sphere it is always, finally, up to us to decide what moral principles are valid and how they apply to particular situations. This claim is often made as a conceptual thesis about the nature of morality or about the nature of moral agents.

To fail to form one's own moral opinions, solve one's own moral problems, make one's own decisions, is to fail as a moral agent.[2]

[A] man faced with such a problem [a moral one – GD] knows that it is his problem and that nobody can answer it for him.[3]

R. M. Hare also formulates the view as one about the freedom of the moral agent: "One of the most important constituents of our freedom, as moral agents, is the freedom to form our own opinions about moral questions, even if that involves changing our language."[4] Aiken takes a similar view: "As a moral being he must

1 Compare Chapter 3.
2 Marcus Singer, "Freedom From Reason," *Philosophical Review* 79 (April 1970), 255.
3 R. M. Hare, *Freedom and Reason* (London: Oxford University Press, 1965), 1.
4 Ibid., 2.

49

also, in principle, be free to decide absolutely for himself what the law really is."[5]

The question that all these quotations raise is, In what sense are moral agents free or unfree to decide upon the correctness of moral principles in a way in which they are not free or unfree to decide upon the correctness of any other proposition? Hare puts the contrast in the following strong terms:

It might be objected that moral questions are not peculiar in this respect – that we are free also to form our own opinions about such matters as whether the world is round . . . but we are free to form our own moral opinions in a much stronger sense than this. For, if we say that the world is flat, we can, in principle, be shown certain facts such that, once we have admitted them, we cannot go on saying that the world is flat without being guilty of self-contradiction or misuse of language . . . nothing of the sort can be done in morals.[6]

It is clear why Hare believes this. He has already accepted a thesis about the autonomy of morals, which is that we cannot derive a moral or normative judgment from a nonnormative or factual judgment. With respect to factual judgments, once one has admitted certain facts, then one has to admit whatever follows from those facts. But there are no facts from which we have to accept the truth of any nonfactual or evaluative judgments. Because we are not compelled to accept the normative judgment, then we are free to accept it or not. Hence, the autonomy of moral agents is a consequence of the autonomy of morals.

As a general view about any moral question or any factual question this view is mistaken. With respect to factual matters, or at least those whose truth depends on some evidence or reasoning as opposed to mere observation, the view is wrong on two grounds. First, there is the point that being shown certain facts does not force us to admit or accept them, and so the hypothetical, even if valid, cannot force us to accept the consequent. It might be that if I accepted the fact that this man is mortal, I must accept the fact that some men are mortal; but why am I not free to refuse to accept the fact that this man is mortal? If it is objected that it is not rational for me to ignore evidence relevant to the truth of a proposition whose truth-value I am uncertain about, then it may be replied that

5 H. D. Aiken, *Reason and Conduct* (New York: Alfred A. Knopf, 1962), 142.
6 Hare, *Freedom and Reason*, 2.

it is not rational for me to ignore those considerations which provide reasons for or against accepting some moral proposition.

But, more significantly, with facts of any moderate complexity, no set of facts that are not logically equivalent to them forces me to accept their truth. Consider the very example that Hare uses: that of the roundness of the earth. This is a nonobservational fact that must be inferred from a set of observations together with a set of physical laws; the whole package constituting an explanation of the original set of facts. The roundness of the earth does not follow from other facts; it is the best explanation of them. As philosophers from Duhem to Quine have argued, it is always possible to maintain that an alternative explanation gives a better account of the facts. Now it is true that it may require ad hoc and silly hypotheses in order to maintain that another explanation is as good, but those who put forward silly and ad hoc views are not guilty of the two sins of which Hare accuses them. They are not guilty of contradicting themselves or of misusing language. Perhaps they are violating certain canons of rational practice, but because these are normative in character, by Hare's own views they are not required to abide by them unless they choose to.

Note the other side of this coin. It is at least as plausible that to deny that certain facts commit one to certain moral views is a misuse or abuse of language. To admit that I ran over your child deliberately, without excuse or justification, because I disliked you and your child, and to admit all this while maintaining that what I did is morally right, is either a misunderstanding of what moral rightness is, or we will be able to find other moral judgments I make which are inconsistent with this one.

I

The immediate problem is to give a characterization of moral autonomy that at least, prima facie, does appear to differentiate our acceptance of moral judgments from those of some contrast class – preferably scientific judgments.

The essence of the thesis is a connection between the authority or bindingness of moral judgments on a person and their acceptance or acknowledgment. A conceptual connection is asserted between the acknowledgment of a moral principle and its being authoritative. A corollary of all this is the denial of moral authority. All

51

these connections are supposed to be different in the case of non-moral judgments.

> No one can be expected to conform his judgment and his will to certain alleged objective principles which he has not in conscience made absolutely his own... [an] authority can make no moral claims upon anyone who does not adopt it as his authority.[7]

> The moral agent may learn from others about his moral obligations, but only in the sense that a mathematician learns from other mathematicians – namely, by hearing from them arguments whose validity he recognizes even though he did not think of them himself. He does not learn in the sense that one learns from an explorer, by accepting as true his accounts of things one cannot see for oneself.[8]

I have already argued against this view in Chapter 3. To the limited extent that we are taught about morality we do rely on others to see what we cannot yet recognize.

In any case, it is quite clear that much of what we learn about the moral life is not acquired in any conscious and deliberate fashion. We imitate exemplary individuals, follow the reasoning and perceptions of persons who are significant and important to us, and we learn far more than we are taught. This is as true, say, for our acquisition of language as for our moral reasoning. If there is a notion of authority here, it is authority of the deed and not of the word.

So far I have argued that there are certainly cases in which it makes sense to think of one relying upon the advice and judgment of others in moral matters. I now want to point out how a version of the autonomy thesis is plausible as an account of what justifies authority in science. For the notion of scientific authority rests upon the acceptance and acknowledgment of canons of evidence, of ideals of explanation, of norms of theory construction, and of norms of relevance. Nothing forces a scientist to accept one rather than another of these presuppositions for the idea of authority making sense. Thus, one could argue that there is freedom to form our own opinions about factual questions, although the existence of this freedom is concealed by the fact that there is fairly widespread agreement about the preconditions for authoritative judgment in various areas of empirical knowledge. Indeed, one might say that

7 Aiken, *Reason and Conduct*, 143.
8 R. P. Wolff, *In Defense of Anarchism* (New York: Harper & Row, 1970), 7.

it is the existence of this consensus which demarcates, at least descriptively, science from pseudoscience.

Consider, for example, what a scientific dispute among the following might look like: a quantum mechanic, a Christian Scientist, an astrologer, a psychiatrist, and a phrenologist. In the absence of shared norms about what counts as explanation of what good science is, of the criteria that are relevant to the acceptance or rejection of theories, of the weight to be attached to competing criteria, of the importance of conflicting observations or thought experiments, it will look very much as if it is up to each person to form his own judgment about the "facts."[9] There will be no notion of authority other than the kind of thing Henry Aiken suggests when he says that authority can make no claim upon those who do not accept it as authoritative. We would have the epistemological equivalent of existentialism.

It should not be thought that such a difference in norms of inquiry only takes place among what might be called epistemological deviants. If one looks, for example, at the type of criteria that Aristotle and Plato used to evaluate theories, one sees that the history of science is, in part, a history of the development of various evaluative schemes. For them scientific knowledge involves knowing the final causes of events: that for the sake of which they exist. Mechanism and efficient causes are a lower form of knowledge. Hence, different sorts of considerations would be relevant in assessing the truth of scientific theories.

As another instance, consider the following passage from Descartes concerning his two laws of motion:

But even if all that our senses have ever experienced in the actual world would seem manifestly to be contrary to what is contained in these two rules, the reasoning which has led me to them seems so strong that I am quite certain that I would have to make the same supposition in any new world of which I have been given an account.[10]

A dispute between Descartes and a crude empiricist would look very much like a dispute between a Nazi and a Gandhian on the legitimacy of force.

9 Cf. A. Gewirth, "Positive 'Ethics' and Normative 'Science,'" *Philosophical Review* 69 (April 1960), 311–30.
10 Quoted in B. Ellis, "Truth as a Mode of Evaluation," *Pacific Philosophical Quarterly* 61 (1 & 2), 87.

All this is by way of trying to undermine the sharp distinction being drawn between our freedom to choose what to believe or accept in matters moral and in matters factual. It is not to deny that there may be important differences in the range of freedom in the two domains. But exactly what those differences are and their implications for issues of rationality and objectivity in the two realms remains to be clarified.

II

Why has it seemed to so many, and so obviously, that a notion of moral authority is impossible or incoherent? To say that nobody else can make one's moral decisions for one has the form of what Wittgenstein called a "grammatical" remark. It is like saying that nobody else can feel my pain (for then it would be his pain and not mine). Who else could make my decisions? You may, in certain contexts, decide for another, as in the case of a parent who volunteers his child for a medical experiment. But then, quite clearly, the child has made no decision. To decide for somebody is not to make his decision. In this sense nobody else can make my medical or financial or career decisions for me. There is nothing special about moral decisions.

But I might consent to having somebody else make my moral decisions for me. I might simply accept whatever decision they would make and, therefore, let them make my decision. If X said that humility is a virtue, I would believe humility is a virtue. If he said I should do this thing, I would do this thing. It seems that something is wrong here in a way in which something comparable would not be wrong in scientific matters. If I am uncertain about the correct statistical test to use, or what the pain in my leg is, or why the thermostat is not working, or the number of words for "snow" that the Eskimo have, then I consult an authority. As Aiken puts it:

In the domain of science and logic . . . situations often arise in which we properly defer to the authority of observers whom we recognize to be more competent or qualified than ourselves. And it is because of that, without qualms, we accept certain statements as objectively true even though we ourselves do not fully see whey they are so. But in morals such situations can hardly arise . . . [11]

11 Aiken, *Reason and Conduct*, 143.

Again, I want to call attention to the extent to which this picture is not accurate in either morals or science. With respect to morality, it is certainly the case that for much of human history, and for most persons, to determine what was right was to consult authorities – whether priests or the elders or the learned. To say that such a practice is not a morality is either to adopt a stipulative definition of morality or to maintain a substantive thesis about the "correct" or "rational" way in which to think about moral matters.

It is interesting to compare the making of moral judgments with aesthetic judgment. Although they are both evaluative, although there is much disagreement about particular cases in both areas, the notion of authority has never drawn the same critical fire in aesthetics. And, correspondingly, there has not been the same emphasis on the individual as being free to choose his own aesthetic principles or standards. Thus, there has been more acceptance of the role of the expert who guides us in our perception of aesthetic objects, who calls attention to the relevant features of the object, who has more experience in such matters.

Certainly someone who made no effort to test the views of experts in her own experience, who made no effort to develop her own taste in aesthetic matters, would be thought aesthetically shallow. But a mathematics student would be thought mathematically shallow who merely accepted the word of her teacher that such and such a theorem is true without tying to discover, or at least verify the proof of the theorem.

Without making the strong claim that matters are on a par in science and morals, one can argue that authority has some role in both. As E. Anscombe points out, there is a sort of authority that can hardly be denied to exist by "the most recalcitrant modern philosopher. For it is exercised by people in bringing up their children . . . "[12] And, as S. Toulmin says:

When we say "it is known that so-and-so" or "biochemistry tells us that so-and-so" . . . we do not mean that everyone knows, or that every biochemist will tell us that so-and-so. We normally imply rather that this is the 'authoritative' view – both in the disciplinary sense, i.e., the view supported by the best accredited body of experience, and also in the profes-

12 E. Anscombe, "Authority in Morals," *Concepts in Social and Political Philosophy*, ed. R. E. Flathman (New York: Macmillan, 1973), 157.

sional sense, i.e., the view supported by the influential authorities in the subject.[13]

III

Suppose we consider the following notion of moral autonomy. A person is morally autonomous if he:

cannot accept without independent consideration the judgment of others as to what he should do. If he relies on the judgment of others, he must be prepared to advance independent reasons for thinking their judgment likely to be correct.[14]

The idea of there being independent reasons for thinking the judgment of an authority correct is ambiguous. There are reasons for thinking his *judgment* likely to be correct, that is, independent reasons for believing the specific content of his judgment. Or, there can be independent reasons for thinking *his* judgment to be correct, or, in other words, for thinking *him* likely to be right.

It is certainly true that there are many occasions in science where we do not insist that we have independent grounds for supposing the particular content of what an authority says is true. The same is true when we seek practical advice from experts, for example, my doctor's opinion on what medicine I should take. There are obvious reasons why the institution of science, and more generally our factual knowledge should dispense with the requirement of independent checks on authority. We often lack the time, training, skill, and prior knowledge needed to make such checks. It is efficient for each of us to specialize in a few areas of competence and to draw when needed upon the resources and expertise of others. Knowledge is socially stored and there are evolutionary advantages for a species that does not require each member to acquire and retain all knowledge needed for survival and reproduction. Insofar as moral knowledge is advantageous to the species we should expect a similar division of labor there as well.

My conclusion at this point is that any strong claim about differences concerning autonomy in science and morality must rely not on a conceptual point about the nature of moral reasoning, but

---

13 S. Toulmin, *Human Understanding* (New Jersey: Princeton University Press, 1972), 264.
14 T. Scanlon, "A Theory of Freedom of Expression," *Philosophy and Public Affairs* 1 (Winter 1972), 216. This is not put forward by Scanlon as a conception of *moral* autonomy.

on a substantive ideal of the moral agent as a critical and self-conscious actor. One way of evaluating that ideal is by examining its implications for various theoretical ideals. One such ideal is that of objectivity, and I propose to discuss the compatibility of an autonomy-based moral theory with the notion of objectivity.

IV

It is clear that different moral theories will have different conceptions of what is involved in being morally autonomous. Let me just briefly illustrate the range of notions.[15] On the Kantian view, autonomy is a property of the will of moral agents that allows them to act on principles and not be determined by empirical causes. We commit ourselves to moral principles by reason alone. On the Sartrean, or Hareian, view moral principles are chosen freely, are self-imposed, and cannot be given a more ultimate justification. On the Rawlsian view, the parties making a hypothetical choice of principles are characterized as autonomous in the sense that they "are moved solely by their highest-order interests in their moral powers and by their concern to advance their determinate but unknown final ends."[16] In addition, the actual acceptance of principles of justice in a well-ordered society is via a theoretical argument about the original position, so that their acceptance of the principles of justice expresses their conception of themselves as autonomous and equal citizens.

I take it that the root idea of all these conceptions is a notion of morality as constructed rather than discovered, as chosen rather than imposed. Rawls puts the view this way:

Apart from the procedure of constructing the principles of justice, there are no moral facts. Whether certain facts are to be recognized as reasons of right and justice, or how much they are to count, can be ascertained only from within the constructive procedure; that is, from the undertakings of rational agents of construction when suitably represented as free and equal moral persons.[17]

15 I am relying in part on distinctions made by Thomas Hill, Jr. in "Autonomy and Benevolent Lies," *Journal of Value Inquiry* 18 (No. 4, 1984), 251–67.
16 J. Rawls, "Kantian Constructivism in Moral Theory," *Journal of Philosophy*, 77 (September 1980), 525.
17 Ibid., 519.

Such autonomy-based theories must abandon the idea of the truth of moral principles, or at the least, claim that their being true is not the source of their validity for the agent. As usual, Rawls is clear about the implications of his meta-theory.

> Given the various contrasts between Kantian constructivism and rational intuitionism, it seems better to say that in constructivism first principles are reasonable (or unreasonable) than that they are true (or false).[18]

Given that such theories dispense with a claim to truth, what role does the notion of objectivity play within such theories? There is also the further question of an account of objectivity when applied to questions about what to do as opposed to what to believe. Let me begin by considering the question of objectivity as applied to theoretical reasoning.

Ultimately the distinction between appearance and reality lies at the heart of questions concerning objectivity. Issues of objectivity arise when we suppose that there is a difference between how things *seem* to us, and how they *really* are. As the terminology of appearance and reality indicates, metaphors of perception are dominant. We are aware that we confront experience from within a certain perspective and that attempts to gain knowledge are conditioned in various ways by the place from which we start. Once we become aware of the possibility of distortion, we seek, by gaining an understanding of distorting factors, to arrive at a perspective that is more likely to bring us closer to the way things are.

There are well-known and deep philosophical difficulties associated with the idea of objectivity. Even if we understand the thought of escaping from an idiosyncratic and partial perspective to a more universal and complete one, there always remains the worry of how we are able to jump out of our own skins. For the effort to transcend our own point of view is always launched from within some point of view of our own. I do not intend to solve those problems here; for one reason because one cannot intend to do what one is not able to do. For my purposes it is sufficient to present the ideal of objectivity as fashioned for theoretical reasoning and to see if there is an analogue for theories of practical reasoning, particularly those that do not appeal to a notion of truth.

18 Ibid., 569.

As Anscombe once put it, the point of practical reasoning is to make the world fit my thought rather than to match my thought to the world. Still there ought to be reasons to justify making the world one way rather than another. In the case of some branches of practical reasoning, for example, prudence, these reasons will have reference to the ends of the agent and the best ways of securing them. For prudential theorizing objectivity will be tied to certain practical tasks that a theory of prudence enables us to perform better or worse than alternative theories. Once we have an idea of what we want prudential theories for, we will know how to evaluate such theories as better or worse (in an objective sense.)[19]

A similar view has been taken with respect to moral reasoning. It has been characterized as an attempt to contribute to the amelioration of the human condition or to enable many persons to solve coordination problems or to promote the general good or to overcome the limitations of self-interest. I myself think that any attempt to find *a* substantive "point" or "purpose" for moral reasoning is mistaken, not least because paying attention to the historical facts shows how varied such tasks have been.[20]

Still I think that in a given historical and philosophical context one can say something illuminating about how moral discussion and theorizing is viewed at a given time, and what one might want a moral theory for so that, *relative* to a particular set of practical tasks, one can have a notion of objectivity that is independent of the idea of truth.

For us, now, moral reasoning takes place in a context of seeking to find and provide reasons that will have general scope and appeal. An important motivation for moral discussion arises from our desire to justify what we propose to do, or have done, to others. The importance of this idea of interpersonal justification in contemporary moral philosophy can be seen by noting the common element in various tests that have been proposed by moral philos-

---

19 Cf. D. Parfit, *Reasons and Persons* (Oxford: Oxford University Press, 1984) for discussions along these lines.
20 Compare, for example, Schneewind's view that in the seventeenth and eighteenth centuries the role of a moral code was to provide us with adequate instruction about the role that we were to play in God's plans for the cosmos. And the role of the moral theorist was to explain what the laws of morality were and to explain how we receive adequate guidance from them. "The Divine Corporation and the History of Ethics," in *Philosophy in History*, eds. R. Rorty, J. Schneewind, Q. Skinner (Cambridge: Cambridge University Press, 1984).

ophers: Hare's test of whether one could prescribe for oneself what one prescribes for others, Rawls's unanimity behind the veil of ignorance, Nagel's view that one must be able to justify – to another person – what one does to that person, and most recently (and most fully developed) Scanlon's defense of contractualism viewed as the attempt to find agreement among those who are motivated by this very desire.[21] This search for a standpoint from which the existence of other independent, equal moral agents is given full weight is the equivalent of that search for that distance from one's own perspective on the universe which defines objectivity for theoretical reasoning.

This view of objectivity is compatible with, although it does not require, the denial of truth value to moral judgments. The constraints on what is acceptable are practical. On the view being advanced here, one role of moral theory is to secure convergence in judgment, agreement by moral agents as to what should be done in particular situations. Part of the "verification" of a theory is a prediction that, over time, judgments will tend to converge. Convergence, however, is neither necessary nor sufficient for "practical" objectivity. It is not sufficient, for the explanation of the convergence may be in terms of relatively external and superficial features of human psychology, for example, brain-washing or manipulation. It is not necessary because we have similar kinds of explanations for nonconvergence, for example, structures of exploitation may make it impossible for those in power to reason soundly.

Another set of constraints is connected with what it feels like to live by certain moral codes or to attempt to live by them. One of the values of great literature is being confronted by vivid pictures of what it is like to live by certain codes, or to seek to manifest certain virtues, or to be faced with the moral dilemmas that are raised by accepting certain ideals. Moral codes are connected with ways of living and with ideals of human flourishing. The attempt to live by certain moralities or to rehearse what that would be like is the analogue to observational testing of scientific theories. "Try it, you'll like it" is a reasonable criterion for a moral theory.

Being capable of holding up against various kinds of rational

21 T. Scanlon, "Contractualism and Utilitarianism," in *Beyond Utilitarianism*, eds. A. Sen, B. Williams (Cambridge: Cambridge University Press 1984), 103–28.

criticism, helping us to avoid moral dilemmas, leading to convergence in judgment, proving satisfying, all of these are tasks that a theory can perform better or worse, objectively considered. All of these are tasks that may be performed by moral theories that are viewed as created or constructed rather than discovered, and that therefore are grounded in a conception of autonomy.

To the question of whether scientific objects are real, Wilfred Sellars once replied: "The correct answer is that we invent them and discover that they do the work which we require of something that is to count as real."[22]

The parallel view of moral principles is that we construct them and then discover that they do the work of something that is to count as a correct moral principle.

22 W. Sellers, "Is Scientific Realism Tenable?," in *Proceedings of the 1976 Philosophy of Science Association*, eds. F. Suppe, W. Asquith, 2 (1977), 312.

5

Is more choice better than less?

> One's own free unfettered choice, one's own caprice – however wild it may be... What man wants is simply *independent* choice, whatever that independence may cost and wherever it may lead.
>
> Dostoyevsky, *The Brothers Karamazov*

> In possibility everything is possible. Hence in possibility one can go astray in all possible ways.
>
> Kierkegaard, *The Sickness unto Death*

In recent years the use of ways of thinking practiced by economists has provided the theoretical apparatus for attempting to clarify and resolve normative problems in a number of different areas of social policy. Among the areas in which fruitful work has been done are tort theory, voting behavior, constitutional choice, criminal justice, and the theory of property rights. At the same time, of course, economists have applied the tools of welfare economics to problems of allocation of resources in areas such as education, health, consumer choice, insurance, and natural resources. In all these areas – both traditional and new – there are two kinds of tasks at issue. One is the descriptive one of trying to explain various phenomena – why rules of liability are the way they are, or why they change over time, why a system of private property arose, why individuals make certain choices in the marketplace. The other task is to provide assistance in answering various normative questions – should manufacturers of various products be held strictly liable for accidents caused by defects? Ought blood to be collected on a market or volunteer basis? Should gasoline be rationed or should prices be

This chapter was originally published in *Midwest Studies in Philosophy*, vol. 7, ed. P. French (Minneapolis: University of Minnesota Press, 1982), 47–61. Reprinted by permission.

allowed to rise until the market is cleared? Ought income to be redistributed? Should need alone determine the distribution of medical care? Is it better to have a volunteer or conscript army? What justifies a progressive rate of taxation on incomes? Ought people to be compensated for losses arising from externalities in the existing system of property rights? These are all important and difficult problems, and a mode of analysis that promises us help – if not solutions – in thinking about them is surely to be welcomed.

It would seem, however, that a mode of analysis that has normative implications must contain, either explicitly or implicitly, normative assumptions. Economists, who are well aware of this, have been better than most theorists in trying to make explicit exactly what their criteria of better and worse are, and the states of affairs to which they attribute value. I wish in this essay to examine an assumption that plays a key role in many policy debates but which has received little critical scrutiny – the view that for the rational individual more choices are always preferable to fewer.

Let me first give some examples of how this postulate is used to argue for various policy decisions:

Gordon Tullock uses the principle in an argument justifying the inheritance of wealth.[1] Assuming as a normative criterion Pareto optimality (someone is made better off and no one is made worse off), Tullock argues that the wealth holder is made better off because he has an option that he would not have if inheritances were not allowed.

A similar argument is made by economists to argue the superiority of income redistribution by means of cash transfers rather than "in kind" provision of various goods, such as food stamps or medical care. The argument again relies on the view that if the recipients receive cash, they can spend it on the particular good in question or choose an alternative expenditure; whereas they have no such choice if they receive the good itself.[2]

---

1 Gordon Tullock, "Inheritance Justified," *Journal of Law and Economics* 14 (1971), 465.
2 This, of course, is true only if no subsequent trade is possible. But, in the case of many goods considered for redistribution (education, health), this is usually the case. See E. O. Olsen, "Some Theorems in the Theory of Efficient Transfers,"

Again, with respect to the issue of how blood should be collected, Kenneth Arrow argues against Richard Titmuss's claim that blood should not be purchased.

Economists typically take for granted that since the creation of a market increases the individual's area of choice, it therefore leads to higher benefits. Thus, if to a voluntary blood system we add the possibility of selling blood, we have only expanded the individual's range of alternatives. If he derives satisfaction from giving, it is argued, he can still give, and nothing has been done to impair that right.[3]

The most explicit statement of the assumption on the theoretical level is that of Gordon Tullock. In a chapter titled "Fundamental Assumptions," his third "basic postulate" is that "an individual would prefer to be permitted to choose . . . that an individual would always prefer to have his range of choices widened."[4]

The view that more choices are preferable to fewer is shared not only by economists but also by many political philosophers. Interestingly, it is shared by philosophers who come to rather different conclusions on substantive matters. Thus, both John Rawls and Robert Nozick accept the thesis.

Rawls classifies liberty as a primary good, that is, one that any rational person will prefer more of to less. His reasoning is that individuals "are not compelled to accept more if they do not wish to, nor does a person suffer from a greater liberty."[5] Nozick uses the claim as part of an argument designed to distinguish offers from threats in terms of their effects on liberty. His contention is that a "rational man would be willing to move and to choose to move from the preoffer to the offer situation, whereas he would normally not be willing to move or to choose to move from the prethreat situation to the threat situation."[6] This is equivalent to assert-

Journal of Political Economy 79 (January/February), 166–76. For a counterview, see Lester Thurow, "Government Expenditures: Cash or In-Kind Aid?" in *Markets and Morals*, eds. G. Dworkin, G. Bermant, P. Brown, (Washington, D.C.: Hemisphere, 1977), 85–106.

3 Kenneth Arrow, "Gifts and Exchanges," *Philosophy and Public Affairs* (Summer 1972), 19–50.
4 Gordon Tullock, *The Logic of the Law* (New York: Basic Books, 1971), 15, 18.
5 John Rawls, *A Theory of Justice*, Cambridge, Mass., Harvard, 1972, p. 143.
6 Robert Nozick, "Coercion," in *Philosophy, Politics, and Society*, 4th series, eds. P. Lasslett, W. Runciman (Oxford: Oxford University Press, 1967), 132. Although Nozick believes there are exceptions, he thinks that all such cases can be analyzed

ing that a rational person always prefers to be offered expanded choices.

What I propose in this essay is to discuss, as John Stuart Mill put it with respect to another "obvious" principle (each person is the best judge of his or her own interests), "the very large and conspicuous exceptions" to this principle.[7] By doing so, we shall not only determine more exactly the limits of the principle, but also, it is hoped, achieve a better understanding of its justification in those situations in which it does apply.

Let me begin by trying to make clearer the nature of the thesis. First, when one speaks of more choices the idea is that one has an original set of options (which may be zero) and at least one more is added. We are not considering the case where we have some (partially) disjoint set which happens to have a larger number of choices than the first. Obviously, having a choice between the Budapest and the Guaneri is preferable to a choice among all the amateur string quartets in New York City.

Next, it does not count against the thesis if additional choices make it less likely that one will get what one wants. Thus, if one is faced with the two doors behind which are the famous lady and the tiger, one does not want one's choices increased by adding three more doors behind all of which are tigers. We are only concerned with options, each of which is known to the chooser.

Finally, the thesis must be understood as having some implicit other-things-being-equal clause. Suppose, for example, A says to B that if B is offered more options with respect to some matter, A will kill B. Here what makes B shun additional choices has nothing to do with the nature of the choices or the nature of choosing, but rather an arbitrary cost attached to the increase in choices. The presence of this cost is too contingent to count against the choices.

I shall present cases in which more choice is not necessarily to be desired and where the connection between the additional choices and the "costs" reflects either general features of choice or intrinsic features of particular choices.

in terms of a special context or the presence of some extraneous reasons. Cf. Dworkin, "Acting Freely," *Nous* (No. 4, 1970), 367–83.
7 J. S. Mill, *Principles of Political Economy*, Vol. 2 (New York: P.F. Collier & Sons, 1900), 448.

In much of the recent economic literature attention has been focused on the concept of transaction costs. It is now generally recognized that the formation and perpetuation of various forms of market exchange are not costless. And the size of such costs must enter into an assessment of whether markets or other forms of resource allocation are most efficient. It should also be recognized that the making of choices is not a costless activity, and the assessment of whether one's welfare is improved by having a wider range of choices is often dependent upon an assessment of the costs involved in having to make these choices.

The kinds of costs are quite varied, and I am going to suggest some samples rather than a well-worked-out typology. One of the most obvious costs is that of acquiring the information required to make reasonable choices – for the notion of rationality is tied very closely to the notion of a well-informed choice. The proliferation of products, services, and so forth, hailed with much enthusiasm as the chief virtue of competitive markets, brings with it the need to know more and more in order to make intelligent choices. Henry Ford was said to have offered his customers a choice of colors – black. This undoubtedly restricted the range a customer had to choose from, but it also eliminated the need to answer questions such as: Which color is the safest in terms of visibility? Which color is likely to show the least dirt? Which color is my spouse likely to prefer? Which color will "last" in terms of fashion, etc.?

The example is a trivial one. When it comes to questions of product safety, or a doctor's competence, or the consequences of going to a particular college, the issues become more serious, the information more difficult to obtain, and the costs of acquiring the information higher.[8]

In addition to the costs of acquiring relevant information, there are the costs in time and effort of making the choice. Anybody who has tried to buy a house or a car will be aware of the time-consuming nature of these choices. And although one can trade off

8 There are various ways in which the law may eliminate the need for acquiring information. One can embody certain information in the product itself, for example, by setting product standards. Or, by banning products from the market, the consumer can be spared the task of making comparisons!

money for time by hiring agents to do the initial screening, location, and other tasks involved, the nature of the choice dictates a necessary investment of personal time. One does not want to live in a house picked out by a real-estate agent.[9]

There are, in addition, the psychic costs of having made the decision. Was this really the right house or college or doctor? If I had waited, would I have had a better selection, a cheaper price? Because it's my choice, how does it reflect on me? This last worry brings us to the next category of reasons that weigh on the side of preferring fewer choices – the issue of responsibility.

At the most fundamental level, responsibility arises when one acts to bring about changes in the world as opposed to letting fate or change or the decisions of other actors determine the future. Indeed, once I am aware that I have a choice, my failure to choose now counts against me. I now can be responsible, and be held responsible, for events that prior to the possibility of choosing were not attributable to me. And with the fact of responsibility comes the pressure (social and legal) to make "responsible" choices.

Let us consider a specific instance which has arisen recently. Medical advances have made it possible, by the technique of amniocentesis, to determine whether the fetus a woman bears is normal or is genetically deficient in a number of ways. Conjoined with this new knowledge has come the removal of legal restrictions on the right of a woman to have an abortion – at least in the first twenty-four weeks of gestation. These two circumstances now imply that if parents bring, say, a Down's syndrome infant into the world, they bear the responsibility for this action; a responsibility that could not be attributed to them prior to the possibility of determining the normality of the fetus and the legal possibility of terminating the pregnancy. Now, both in their own mind and in the minds of those who are aware of their decision, they must

9 One of the roles of social conventions (forms of greeting, modes of acceptable dress) is to eliminate the necessity of making choices. Wittgenstein is said to have told his landlady that he did not care what he had for breakfast as long as it was the same every day.

assume responsibility for the correctness of the choice. The defective child – if they choose to bear it – can no longer be viewed as inevitable bad luck or as an act of God or as a curse.

Without going to the metaphysical leap of a "fear of freedom," we can on a more sober level accept the fact that more choices bring in their train more responsibility, and that these are costs that must be taken into account. It may be that the willingness to accept responsibility for one's acts is a sign of moral maturity, but this is consistent with the burdensome quality of accepting such responsibility. In addition to bearing the responsibility in one's own mind, there arises the possibility of being held responsible.[10]

PRESSURE TO CONFORM

The fact that one has new possibilities for choice opens the possibility of social and legal sanctions being brought to bear on the maker of the choice. Consider the possibility of predetermining the sex of one's children.

This possibility is now at hand in a negative fashion – amniocentesis plus abortion of the fetus if it is of the undesired sex – and will soon be possible in a positive fashion (techniques for separating the male-producing sperm from female ones). Leaving aside for the moment the question of the adverse effects on society such choices might cause – the available evidence from surveys of parental preference is that a surplus of males would be produced – consider the social pressures that are likely to be exerted on parents to produce one sex rather than the other (the grandparents who always wanted a little girl, or the community that needs more soldiers).

A rather different example of the same phenomenon occurred in many university communities with respect to the issue of coed dormitories and cohabitation. The traditional libertarian response to this question has been a reference to freedom of choice. Those

10 See the reasoning behind one court's decision to force a Jehovah's Witness to have a life-saving blood transfusion. The court argued, on a fine point of theology, that the religious freedom of the patient was not inhibited because it was the choice of blood, not the blood itself, that was forbidden. Application of the President and Directors of Georgetown College, 331 F. 2d 1000 (D.C. Cir.), Cert denied, 377 U.S. 978, 1964. William Powers reminded me of this decision.

who wish to cohabit now can, whereas those who do not wish to can continue in their (old-fashioned?) ways. The opening of new options cannot be harmful and is beneficial to some. But this is to ignore the sociology of the situation. The obvious reply – which came fairly quickly from those who felt the pressures of their peers – is that by allowing cohabitation, the social pressures from one's peers to act in a similar fashion increases and the easy excuse formerly available to those not so inclined vanishes. Similarly, one of the justifications for making dueling illegal is that unless this is done, individuals might be forced to manifest their courage and integrity in ways that they would wish to avoid.

As another example, consider the argument of Tullock that allowing the inheritance of wealth is a Pareto optimal policy.[11] Leaving aside the obvious objections (the inequality of opportunity, etc.) which he considers, there is the objection that the wealth holder herself may be worse off by having the option. She might prefer to spend all her wealth on herself and leave none to her heirs. A law that denies her the option of leaving her money to others frees her from the expectations and pressures of others.

I am not now arguing that the existence of various pressures to conform should be taken as decisive in retaining the status quo. It may be argued that, either because people have a right to such increased choices or because it is simply desirable to do so, such pressures have to be tolerated. I am simply pointing out the ways in which increased choices may incur costs. In particular, one of the costs may be, as above, a decrease in the likelihood of exercising previous choices. I turn now to this category.

EXERCISE OF CHOICE

I quoted earlier Arrow's argument in favor of allowing a market for blood: "[I]f to a voluntary blood donor system we add the possibility of selling blood, we have only expanded the individual's range of alternatives. If he derives satisfaction from giving, . . . he can still give, and nothing has been done to impair that right."[12] Titmuss in his essay on the subject of blood, "The Gift Relation-

11 Tullock, "Inheritance Justified."
12 Arrow, "Gifts and Exchanges."

ship," argues that this is false. The argument is not a clear one, and it is worth some time pursuing it since the general point is relevant to our topic. Titmuss states that

> private market systems in the United States and other countries not only deprive men of their freedom to choose to give or not to give, but by so doing escalate other coercive forces in the social system which lead to the denial of other freedoms . . .
> We believe that policy and processes should enable men to be free to choose to give to unnamed strangers. They should not be coerced or constrained by the market.[13]

The question that Arrow raises is how can expanding choices decrease them? How can being free to give or sell blood constitute a less free system than one in which one can only give blood (or for that matter, only sell)? Peter Singer seems to interpret Titmuss's claim as being one about the liberty to give a certain kind of gift.

> The right that Titmuss says is threatened is not a simple right to give, but the right to give "in non-material as well as material ways." This means not merely the right to give money for some commodity that can be bought or sold for a certain amount of money, but the right to give something that cannot be bought, that has no cash value, and must be given freely if it is to be obtained at all. This right, if it is a right – it would be better to say, this freedom – really is incompatible with the freedom to sell, and we cannot avoid denying one of these freedoms when we grant the other.[14]

So freedom is diminished because prior to the introduction of the freedom to sell we were free to give something that cannot be purchased. Now we are only free to give something that can be purchased as well.

The argument strikes one as paradoxical. Suppose in a certain prison mail could go out only after being read by a censor. New regulations allow prisoners a choice of sending their mail out in the accustomed fashion or unread by a censor. Surely we would regard this as an expansion of freedom. Yet, a Singerian argument could be constructed to show that whereas previously a prisoner could send a letter knowing it would be read by the censor, now the nature of the prisoner's letter is altered. The recipient of the

---

13 Richard Titmuss, *The Gift Relationship* (New York: Pantheon, 1972), 239, 242.
14 Peter Singer, "Freedoms and Utilities in the Distribution of Health Care," in *Markets and Morals*, 163–6.

letter is not guaranteed to have had the letter read by someone other than the writer of the letter. Of course the example is silly because we can think of no reason to want to be assured of this fact. But this seems to show that it is the alteration of the nature of the gift and not the effect on freedom that is crucial.

Another way of putting this point: We are not able to give a gift of a certain kind, and hence the issue of freedom does not arise. If I touch you, I make it impossible for anyone to speak to you while speaking to someone untouched by me. If we allow people to work on the Sabbath, we make it impossible for anyone to work six days a week, and be assured that everyone else will rest on the Sabbath. And people may want to have the assurance, just as they may want to be able to give something that cannot be bought. But we should keep distinct the myriad of ways in which we can make things impossible to do from those very special restrictions that constitute enlarging or restricting freedom.

A more plausible way of defending Titmuss is Peter Singer's later view that the argument should not be formulated in terms of a denial of freedom, but rather in terms of the likely results that the expansion of choice will have on the motivation of individuals to continue to give voluntarily.

The existence of

a commercial system may discourage voluntary donors. It appears to discourage them, not because those who would otherwise have made voluntary donations choose to sell their blood instead if this alternative is available to them (donors and sellers are, in the main, different sections of the population), but because the fact that blood is available as a commodity, to be bought and sold, affects the nature of the gift that is made when blood is donated.

[E]ven if these people had the formal right to give to a voluntary program that existed alongside commercial blood banks, their gift would have lost much of its significance. . . . The fact that blood is a commodity, that if no one gives it, it can still be bought, makes altruism unnecessary, and so loosens the bonds that can otherwise exist between strangers in the community.[15]

Thus, by increasing the options available, one changes the nature of the old options and may, therefore, affect the likelihood of individuals exercising such options.

There are, of course, examples of situations in which it is not

15 Ibid., 161–6.

71

the willingness to exercise choices that is reduced, but the choices themselves. Consider the development of the use of the automobile and its effect on mass transportation. At first the purchase of an automobile greatly expanded the options open to individuals. They could take the bus to work or their car. They were not restricted to the particular schedules of mass transit. But, as more and more people began to take advantage of the enlargement of options, funds were diverted from maintenance and improvement of mass transit to the construction of more and better highways. Powerful lobbies developed which encouraged the development of this process so that eventually many inhabitants of cities found themselves increasingly in the position of having to buy a car to get to work. The option of mass transit or private automobile had, in effect, been closed owing to the decline of the former. What started out as an increase of the area of choice resulted in a situation in which one of the original choices was no longer available. Although such cases are interesting, they are irrelevant to the thesis because we do not have all of the original choices.

One of the main arguments for supposing that more choices are always desirable is that adding additional options cannot make one worse off for one need not exercise any of the new choices. This is to ignore the fact that the possibility of increased choices can affect (for the worse) the original situation.

Consider, for example, marriage as a social institution that may be dissolved (more or less easily) as compared to a situation in which the possibility of dissolution is not present. The presence or absence of this possibility must affect the expectations brought to the marriage, the ability to tolerate imperfections of the marriage partner, the sense of commitment to the marriage. It is surely naive to suppose that the mere presence of a choice which need not be taken cannot alter the initial situation.

As another example, consider the following passage by Tibor Scitovsky:

If, beginning with a situation in which only one kind of shirt were available, a man was transposed to another in which ten different kinds were offered to him, including the old kind, he could of course continue to buy the old kind of shirt. But it does not follow that, if he elects to do this, he is no worse off in the new situation. In the first place, he is aware that he is now *rejecting* nine different kinds of shirts whose qualities he has not compared. The decision to ignore the other nine shirts is itself a cost, and inasmuch as additional shirts continue to come on to the market, and some are withdrawn, he is being subjected to a continual process of decision-making even though he is able, and willing, to buy the same shirt. In the second place, unless he is impervious to fashion, he will feel increasingly uncomfortable in the old shirt. It is more likely that he will be tempted, then, to risk spending an unpredictable amount of time and trouble in the hope of finding a more suitable shirt.[16]

In *The Sickness unto Death*, Kierkegaard refers to the "despair of possibility"; a situation in which possibility "appears to the self ever greater and greater, more and more things become possible. . . . At last it is as if everything were possible – but this is precisely when the abyss has swallowed up the self." Is is true that for the rational among us it is never the case that "the soul goes astray in possibility?"[17]

INCREASED CHOICES AND WELFARE DECLINE

We have been considering cases of the impact of choice-expansion on choice. When the choices lost are considered better or more important or more satisfying than the choices gained, a loss of welfare may have occurred. But welfare can be diminished in other ways than by loss or restriction of choices. I shall consider, briefly, some examples of welfare decline that are of this broader category.

Let me begin by considering an example that on the face of it would provide little reason to expect welfare decline: the choice between free and arranged marriages. Philip Slater points out an interesting consequence of abandoning arranged marriages.

There is probably no arena in which free personal choice is more universally valued than that of marital selection, and certainly much misery and horror resulted from the imposition of cultural norms and parental wishes on reluctant brides and bridegrooms. At the same time it would be difficult to maintain that free choice has brought any substantial increase in marital bliss throughout the land. What was lost when people began to choose their own mates was serendipity. When the choice was made on purely practical, social or economic grounds there was an even chance that one might marry a person whose personality and interpersonal style would necessitate a restructuring of

16 Tibor Scitovsky, *The Joyless Economy* (New York: Oxford University Press, 1976), 98.
17 S. A. Kierkegaard, *Fear and Trembling and the Sickness unto Death*, trans. Walter Lowrie (Garden City, N.Y.: Anchor Press, 1954), 169.

one's own neurotic patterns. The compulsive tendency people now have to reproduce their childhood experiences in their marriages is jarred in such a system by the reality of the other person. While I would never advocate a return to the other system, we should be alert to its advantages as well as its more familiar drawbacks.[18]

Another category of cases where increased choice may bring welfare decline are those where there are strategic reasons for not wanting certain choices to be available. If a bank teller knows the combination to the safe, he can be threatened into opening it. If we have no choice about whether to retaliate against nuclear attack (the "doomsday" machine that responds automatically to our being attacked), then our threat of retaliation is more credible than if we have such a choice.

If we turn to prisoners' dilemma situations, we find an interesting category of adverse consequences of having certain choices. It is well known that one way of avoiding the dilemma is to make it impossible for either party to make their dominant choice. Having fewer choices ensures that they will both be better off. But, it might be replied, what is more desirable for any particular player is that the others be coerced into performing the dominated action while he is left free to perform the dominant one. True enough, but, as is the case for many kinds of social interaction, one often cannot remain exceptional. Some form of universal choice is required. Choices come linked rather than separate, so that the question of whether the individual is to have more choices becomes the same as whether some larger group is to have these choices as well. Although these cases are not, in theory, counterexamples to the thesis, they are so in practice. When considerations of fairness or efficiency or political reality require that our choices be linked, it is impossible to ignore the effect on the individual of others having the additional choices as well.

Failure to fully appreciate this fact undermines Rawls's argument for the status of liberty as a primary good, that is, one that any rational person prefers more of to less. He says that individuals "are not compelled to accept more if they do not wish to, nor does a person suffer from a greater liberty."[19] This is presumably

18 Philip Slater, *Earthwalk* (New York: Harper & Row, 1974), 17.
19 Rawls, *A Theory of Justice*, 143.

on the grounds that we are all to have an equal liberty. But because, as he recognizes, the worth of liberty to various persons is not equal, a larger liberty for all may leave some worse off than a smaller liberty for all.[20] As Hart puts it, "It does not follow that a liberty which can only be obtained by an individual at the price of its general distribution through society is one that a rational person would still want."[21]

There are instances in which it is not the fact that choices are linked which makes it rational for the individual to prefer less choice, but the fact that they are not so linked – that he or she is exceptional. It is not fair for some person to be able to purchase release from a system for conscription, and so we do not allow the option. Again, it is a bad argument to say that it is still preferable from the standpoint of any particular individual to have such an option because, if he is motivated by moral considerations, he can always decline to exercise the option. This misses the point that it is already morally significant that he has the choice – whether or not he intends to make use of it. It is his having the choice, whereas others do not, which is ruled out on moral grounds.

An important kind of consideration, to which little attention has been paid, is the role of restricting choices in symbolizing or expressing moral relationships. Consider, for example, the notion of fidelity in a marriage. By foreclosing in advance the idea of alternative sexual relationships (foreclosing not by declining options but by abandoning the very idea of an option), one can express to one's partner the special character of one's relationship. The abandoning of certain choices provides a way of manifesting in the clearest fashion that the relationship is of a special nature.

This way of manifesting certain ideals can take place on a larger scale. I know of a philosophy department whose members have agreed not to use outside offers to raise their salaries. An individual who might otherwise benefit by use of the market can, by renounc-

20 See my "Non-neutral Principles," *Journal of Philosophy*, 71 (August 15, 1974), 491–506, for an application of this reasoning to the problem of tolerance.
21 H. L. A. Hart, "Rawls on Liberty and Its Priority," *University of Chicago Law Review* 40 (No. 3, 1973), 551.

ing in advance this option, express a certain notion of community solidarity.

Note that in these cases it need not be argued that these are the only ways of expressing such ideas. One can conceive of a community (of philosophers or others) who do not regard their community as undermined by the fact that individuals through either talent or luck are enabled to better their circumstances. But that such commitments are one way of expressing the unique character of a community, and that it may be perfectly rational to do so, cannot be denied.

PATERNALISM

Finally, we come to a set of reasons for rejecting more choices which I have discussed at some length in an earlier paper.[22] These are cases where it is rational for individuals to reject the possibility of making certain choices on the grounds that if the choices were available they would be tempted to make them and they recognize, in advance, that making such choices would be harmful in terms of their long-range interests.[23] The application of this line of reasoning to drug legislation, civil commitment procedures, and social security provisions is obvious.

It need not be supposed that we always fear being swept away by strong emotions when we welcome having choices reduced. We may simply fear mistake or error. I would not want to have a bomb connected to a number I could dial on my phone, because I might dial it by mistake.

---

22 Gerald Dworkin, "Paternalism," *Monist*, 56 (January 1972), 64–84.
23 Rational chickens apparently act similarly. George Ainslie at Harvard has performed the following experiments: Chickens faced with a key that allowed them 1.5 seconds of food if they pecked at it when it turned red, or 4 seconds if they refrained from pecking, pecked. Ainslie then introduced a new contingency. The key would turn white about 11 seconds before it turned red, and if the chickens pecked the key when it was white, this prevented the key from turning red and they would obtain the 4-second reward. A peck on the white key prevented a choice between a small immediate reward and a large delayed one. The chickens pecked the white key about 90 percent of the time it was offered to them. See H. Rachlin, *Introduction to Modern Behaviorism* (San Francisco: W. H. Freemans, 1970), 186–8.

Having said a good deal about the specific kinds of considerations that might lead individuals to prefer not having certain choices to having them, some reservations should be noted.

First, it does not follow that although individuals might (under certain conditions) prefer not to have had a certain choice, that having such a choice they would (or should) refrain from exercising it. It could be rational to exercise the choice for a number of different reasons. It might be dangerous not to. While I might prefer that the speed limit be limited to fifty-five miles per hour, if in fact it is seventy and everyone else is driving at that speed, it might be folly not to exercise my choice on this matter. Considerations of "second-best" might bring it about that, whereas it would be more just for none to have such choices, efforts by individuals to reject such choices (given their presence) might make a bad situation worse. One such example might be that of pacifism. We might regard the ideal situation as one in which no individual has the option of using force to attain his or her ends (even where those ends are self-defense), but, given that some individuals are going to exercise the option of using force in certain situations, for good persons to renounce that option would be to make a bad situation intolerable. It follows from the above that it may be perfectly rational for individuals to resist having certain choices taken away, even if they would have preferred not to have had such liberties in the first place.

Second, although some of my examples involved the state as the instrument of limiting choices, nothing I have said commits me to believing that it is the most appropriate instrument for such purposes. In many cases individuals can work out specific arrangements with friends, or make use of various market mechanisms for restricting choice (contracts), or use ingenious devices (such as the cigarette box with a lock and timer designed by Azrin to reduce smoking). The question of the appropriate mechanism for limiting choices is one that can only be decided given knowledge of the particular choices, the nature of the individuals involved, the administrative costs, and so forth.

Third, and related to this last point, from the fact that in some particular case it would be rational for the agent to have his choice restricted, it does not follow that others may do this for him against his will. Whereas the question of what is in the best interests of the individual is relevant to deciding issues of when coercion is justified, it is by no means conclusive. A decent respect for the autonomy of individuals will lead us to be very wary of limiting choices even when it is in the rational self-interest of the individuals concerned.

By means of various counterexamples I have tried to present a convincing case that the thesis that more choice is always preferable to less is false. I want to close by looking at some of the reasons one might give for valuing choice and to argue that they do not lend support to the thesis.

THE VALUE OF CHOICE

Arguments for the value of choice may rely either on the instrumental value of choices or on the intrinsic value. That is, either the value that attaches to choices because having more choices contributes causally to the obtaining of other good things or the value that attaches to having more choices for its own sake. I shall consider these each in turn.

One of the ways in which increased choice contributes to the welfare of individuals is by increasing the probability that they will satisfy their desires. People want various things – goods and services, status, affection, power, health, security – and their chances of getting these things are often enhanced if they have more options to choose among. My chance of finding a shirt I like is greater if I have ten different shirts to choose among than if I have only two.

This is a contingent fact about the world. If my taste in shirts was such that I were indifferent to their fit, style, color, and other qualities, greater choice would not increase the probability of my satisfying my desires. Similarly, even if I had rather strict requirements in a shirt, but it just so happened that most shirts met those requirements, then again I would not value choice for its contribution to the satisfaction of my desires. But, given the relatively bad fit between people's wishes and the objects of their satisfaction, one is well advised to have a broader rather than narrower range of options. So one reason for wanting choices increased is the belief or hope that among the additional choices there will be something that is preferable to those things that are available among the existing choices.

Suppose, then, that existing choices provided me with items that matched in optimal fashion my preferences. Additional options simply provide the necessity for rejections. Would the instrumental value of increased choices be nil? No, for my preferences may change, and the greater choices may (then) provide me with better means to satisfy my changed preferences. Right now I do not care about the presence or absence of rhubarb on the menu because I detest rhubarb. But I have been known to change my food preferences in the past, and, if they change in favor of rhubarb, I will be glad if rhubarb is an option. In addition, one way in which our preferences change is by noting unused options and trying them experimentally. That's how I discovered I liked scungilli.

There are other reasons of an instrumental nature for preferring more choices. Some people get satisfaction out of exercising choice; thinking about, choosing among, making choices is a source of satisfaction. Therefore, having more choices to exercise will provide increased satisfaction. Another reason for preferring more choice is that one wishes to develop certain character traits, and their development requires that one practice by making choices. If one wants to develop self-confidence, one may have to make choices rather than to remain passive.

A different kind of reason for wanting to make choices is to learn certain things about oneself. If one wants to discover whether one is rash or timid, courageous or cowardly, one can do so only by seeing what kinds of choices one makes in certain situations.

I do not see, however, that such considerations can lend support to anything other than an empirical generalization to the effect that in many (most? almost all?) circumstances we would prefer to be offered more options rather than less because this will usually promote the attainment of desired goods. But this is no more than a rule of thumb, a rough guide to the future based on past experience. In a similar way, one might reason that usually I am better off having more information rather than less. But if someone were to inform me that tomorrow I will be given a piece of new information I had not known before, then I have no firm conviction that this will be a good thing or a bad thing. It will all depend on whether I have some reason for wanting to know this new information – and I can certainly think of lots of reasons why I might be indifferent or even prefer not to know it.

The support of the stronger claim must come from the view that choice has intrinsic value, is desirable for its own sake. For if choice has value just in virtue of being choice, then more of it must have more value. Leaving aside for the moment the antecedent of this claim, what is the logic of this argument? Does it really follow from the fact that having a child is (in part) intrinsically valuable, that having two is (necessarily?) better? It certainly does not follow that if A is intrinsically valuable and B is intrinsically valuable that having A and B together is intrinsically valuable. Let A = listening to a Bach partita and B = listening to a Beethoven string quartet.

In any case, here is a "proof" that having choices cannot be intrinsically valuable. Suppose someone ranks three goods A, B, and C in that order. Then, making certain plausible assumptions about the infinite divisibility of utility, there will be A, B, and C such that the person prefers a choice between B and C to receiving A. This will occur whenever the utility of having a choice between B and C plus the utility of B is greater than the utility of A. This seems to me irrational. Leaving aside some special feature about this particular choice, for example, that somebody promised me $1,000 if I made the choice between B and C, why should I prefer to receive my second-ranked alternative to my first?

What does have intrinsic value is not having choices but being recognized as the kind of creature who is capable of making choices. That capacity grounds our idea of what it is to be a person and a moral agent equally worthy of respect by all. But, of course, that it is better intrinsically to be a creature that makes choices does not imply that it is always an improvement to have more.

There is another noninstrumental value that attaches to being able to make choices, namely, their constitutive value. By this I mean a value that resides neither in the causal effects of making choices nor in the value of choices for their own sake, but as definitive of a larger complex that is itself valued. If one wants to be the kind of person who makes decisions and accepts the responsibility for them, or who chooses and develops a life-plan, then choices are valued not for what they produce nor for what they are in themselves, but as constitutive of a certain ideal of a good life. What makes a life *ours* is that it is shaped by our choices, is selected from alternatives, and therefore choice is valued as a necessary part of a larger complex. But, again, this would at most support the view that, with respect to a certain range of choices, it is desirable to have some options.

I conclude that neither the instrumental nor the noninstrumental value of having choices supports the view that more are always preferable to fewer. In the realm of choice, as in all others, we must conclude – enough is enough.[24]

24 Versions of this paper were read to the philosophy departments of New York University, University of Wisconsin, Northwestern University, University of Florida, University of Minnesota-Duluth, and Georgetown University. It was also given as an address to the Mountain-Plains Philosophical Association and as the Wayne Leys Memorial Lecture at Southern Illinois University. In addition to the members of these audiences, I am grateful to Joshua Rabinowitz, Lawrence Crocker, Richard Kraut, and Jane English for written comments.

PART II

Practice

6

Consent, representation, and proxy consent

INTRODUCTION

The moral and practical issue that is raised by proxy consent is the issue of when one individual may make decisions about, speak for, and represent the interests of another. In the case of a fetus, or a young child, or a mentally retarded person, or an unconscious person, or a person in great mental distress, or a person who has been found "unfit" to perform certain obligations and duties, the individual whose interests are to be secured and rights protected is viewed as not in a position to, not competent to, make certain important decisions. The issue of proxy consent is one of who shall be authorized to make those decisions and what criteria should guide the proxy in making such decisions.

The issue of proxy consent can arise in many different contexts. We might be concerned with the financial responsibility of a senile individual. We might be concerned with the legal powers of a guardian with respect to his or her ward. We might be concerned with who will be best able to look after the interests of a minor child. In this chapter we are primarily concerned with the issue as it arises in the biomedical context, and in particular, as it arises with respect to children and their parents. Thus we are concerned with third-party authority to make decisions about the use of children in medical treatment and research.

I shall examine here the concepts of consent and representation, as they have developed in the context of political authority, to see what implications such concepts might have for the notion of proxy consent. The area of political authority seems a fruitful one in which to begin exploration. In both the political and the biomedical realms

This chapter was originally published in *Who Speaks for the Child?* eds. W. Gaylin and R. Macklin (Hastings-on-Hudson, N.Y.: The Hastings Center, 1982), 191–208. Reprinted by permission.

we have conflicts between the interests of individuals and the interests of some larger group. In both realms we have conflicts between the interests of individuals as they perceive them, and their interests as perceived by others. As a result, in both cases, we find a contrast between moral theories that emphasize individual rights and autonomy, and those theories that emphasize the total good that might be achieved. And in both areas we find questions about eligibility to participate in the process of decision making and about the benefits and costs of the institutions involved. Children and the mentally incompetent are problematic cases in both areas. Finally, and most directly relevant to our concerns here, there are problems about *who* can (may) consent for *whom*. Can my ancestors' consent bind me to obey the state? Can a parent consent for his child to a risky experimental procedure with no direct benefits for the child?

The analogies will not be perfect, for the two areas are similar, not identical. But seeing how and when the analogies fail is itself interesting and illuminating.

CONSENT AND REPRESENTATION

Whenever some persons are thought to have political authority over others the concepts of consent and representation play a crucial role in any theory designed to legitimate or explain this situation. With respect to state authority, the question is: What gives some persons the right to command others, to obligate others to obey such commands, and to enforce such commands by the use of coercion? The answer of political philosophers from Socrates to Rawls has been in terms of some notion of consent. Others may have authority over me if and only if I have granted them that authority. Conversely, I am obligated to obey others only if I have agreed to do so. There must be some voluntary undertaking on my part for any obligation to arise. In Hobbes's words, "there [is] no obligation on anyman which ariseth not from some act of his own."

By consenting, we entitle others to act in ways in which they could not had we not consented. State powers derived from consent are just or legitimate not because they are used in just or benevolent ways, not because they are in the best interests of the governed, but simply because citizens have granted the state those powers.

Closely allied to the notion of consent, but not identical with it, is the idea of representation. In any society, other than the impractical one of unanimous direct democracy, there will be a distinction between the citizens and those who are authorized to make and execute the laws. Some persons will have the right and the responsibility to act for others, to be their agent in the pursuit of their needs or wishes or interests. It is clear in general that the consent of the principal who is being represented is not necessary for his being represented. The existence of various kinds of representation for the incompetent shows this fact. And even if the consent of the principal is sufficient to authorize someone to be his representative there remains the crucial question of what the correct role of the representative ought to be. Ought the representative act as the principal would have acted, or as the principal should have acted, or in the interests of the principal, or in pursuit of his welfare?

I shall first examine some of the varieties of consent that have appeared in the philosophical discussion of political authority. Then I shall argue that the problem of "proxy consent" is not an issue of consent in any straightforward way, but instead an issue of representation. I shall then discuss different ideas of what representation is, and different conceptions of the role of the representative, concluding with some normative remarks about "proxy consent" in the biomedical context, and some problems that need further investigation.

VARIETIES OF CONSENT

The clearest case of consent is actual, explicit consent. If I take a pledge to uphold and maintain the laws of the country I explicitly consent to such authority. If I tell my doctor that he may enroll me in a random controlled clinical trial then there is no question of his justification in doing so, although the fact that he has the right to do so does not preclude the possibility that he ought not to do so on some other grounds.

In the political context two difficulties arose with respect to a theory of explicit consent as the foundation of legitimate authority. Some said that such consent never took place – or at least they never consented. The second difficulty was the view that consent was sometimes not sufficient, and sometimes not necessary to explain legitimate authority.

The first difficulty, that such consent was a fiction, has basically two solutions. The first: The consent really did take place, you just had to know how to find it. The second: It was conceded that it never did occur, but then it was never really supposed to have.

The first solution, introduced by Locke, is that of tacit consent. There is a kind of consent that takes place without the explicit signs that we normally expect as the mark of consent. As Locke puts it:

Every man that hath any possession or enjoyment of any part of the dominions of any government thereby gives his tacit consent, and is as far forth obliged to the laws of that government during such enjoyment, as any one under it, whether this his possession be of land to him and his heirs forever, or lodging only for a week.[1]

The problems with this notion seemed infinite. How does one withdraw one's tacit consent? To what have you consented when you use the roads of a country? The terms of the original contract? The current set of laws?

Whatever its theoretical difficulties it is important for the discussion of proxy consent to distinguish tacit consent from inferred consent (see section below entitled "Proxy Consent"), and these in turn from situations that give rise to obligations as if a person had consented. Tacit consent is no less actual consent for not being explicit. If we think of consent as an act of agreement, a "saying to oneself," then the difference between express and tacit consent is simply the question of whether the individual has made known his consent to others. He may have consented, and the best explanation of his behavior is that he has consented, although he has not expressed it.

Inferred consent, on the other hand, is not actual consent that remains unexpressed. It is simply a judgment about what the agent would have agreed to under certain circumstances. If a surgeon, performing an operation for an ectopic pregnancy, finds an acute appendix and removes it, he will rely on a view about what the patient would have wanted if she had known about the appendix. She did not consent, either explicitly or tacitly, but (it is claimed) she would have. It would be preferable not to call this consent at all, but if we must, then calling it "hypothetical" or "inferred" consent makes the contrast explicit.

The most recent development in political theory is the use of hypothetical consent, rather than actual consent, as the key legiti-

1 John Locke, *The Second Treatise of Government* (New York: Library of Liberal Arts, 1952), 68.

mating factor. Legitimate government is government that deserves consent. It is government that acts within the limits of the authority that rational agents would (under certain ideal conditions) have granted. Actual consent is neither necessary nor sufficient to create obligations to obey governments. For people might consent to obey governments that were unjust and tyrannical, or they might fail to consent to governments that brought benefits to the members of a society that were paid for by some sacrifices by the citizens of the society. Legitimate government is government that deserves consent.

All these should be distinguished from situations in which my behavior gives rise to obligations and expectations *as if* I had consented. My inner denial that I accept the rules of poker will not prevent me from being held to their observance *as if* I had consented. In legal language, I am estopped from using as a defense the fact that I did not consent. This situation has been called quasi-consent.

It is important to see that neither quasi-consent nor hypothetical consent is a species of consent. Neither is a case of consent, but both appeal to consent or something like consent in explaining the obligations and rights they create. To appeal to what a patient (in the ectopic pregnancy case) would have wanted (or to what was in her best interests) is quite different from appealing to her actual consent.

Similarly, proxy consent is not a species of consent. It is precisely when, for various reasons, individuals cannot, do not, or ought not to give their consent that we invoke the notion of proxy consent. In addition the term "proxy," having the connotations of the stockholder's proxy, is misleading. Unlike the stockholder who signs his proxy over to management, and hence explicitly consents to their authority, neither children nor the mentally retarded nor the comatose have expressly abandoned their rights to decide.

Although proxy consent is not a type of consent, the idea of consent is relevant in two ways. First, consent is the background against which delegation of authority stands forward. We only need substitutes when there is a real thing that is lacking. It is because the normal appeal to consent fails that we require a proxy. Second, various theories that attempt to justify the substitution of one person's judgment for another rely on views concerning what the individual whose authority has been delegated would have consented to. This standard will not always hold, for in, say, the case

89

of infants the appeal may be to the interests of the child. But even here there may be lurking in the background a definition of interests in terms of what the child would, on reaching the age of competence, approve or consent to.

The functions that consent serves in the political context are similar to those served in the biomedical area. Consent serves as a check on the power of those agents (political or medical) who are making decisions that affect one's interests in significant ways. Consent makes it more likely that welfare will be maximized because costs are borne only by those willing to pay them and are therefore presumably worth it to those individuals. Consent preserves the autonomy of the individual because his right to self-determination, his control of his body and his possessions, can be abrogated only with his agreement.

However, in both the political and medical contexts it is apparent that consent will not always be possible. In the political realm that is so because we are born into a society with no choice about certain fundamental institutions – which provide the framework within which voluntary transactions can be made and enforced. And short of unanimous, direct democracy these institutions are not such that we can consent to each decision they produce. In the biomedical context, consent fails because of the incompetence of some individuals. In both cases appeal is made to the notion of representation, to the idea that under certain conditions some may speak for and make decisions for others.

REPRESENTATION

There are philosophical differences among political philosophers both about the nature of a representative and about what his role ought to be. Griffiths distinguishes four different notions of representation: descriptive, symbolic, ascriptive, and interest.[2]

A descriptive representative is sufficiently like those he represents that he can be taken as a *sample* on the basis of which one can draw inferences about the represented. As Pitkin puts it, "What qualifies a man to represent is his representativeness – not what he does, but what he is, or is like."[3]

2 A. Phillips Griffiths, "How Can One Person Represent Another?" *Proceedings of the Aristotelian Society* 34 (Supp 1960), 187–208.
3 Hannah Pitkin, *Representation* (New York: Atherton, 1969), 10.

90

Symbolic representation occurs when an individual is taken as a focus for attitudes appropriate to what he is representative of. Thus the queen is the symbol of the English people. Unlike a descriptive representative, a symbolic one need not resemble what he represents in any obvious way.

Someone who has my power of attorney need neither resemble me nor be symbolic of me. Instead he acts in my name and his actions commit me. That is the ascriptive sense of representation.

Finally, someone who represents the oil interests in Congress may not be authorized to do so, nor do his actions commit those interests.

It is worthwhile to note that these competing conceptions of what a representative *is* parallel (with the exception of the notion of symbolic representation) the three explanations given by A. Capron for allowing third-party permission in the law.[4] Corresponding to the idea of a descriptive representative is the "identity-of-interest" doctrine. A proxy is allowed to decide for an incompetent because "the interests of the third party and those of the incompetent are so close that in choosing his or her own interests the third party will choose very much as the incompetent would." The empirical assumption being made here – and it may be as false with respect, say, to a trade unionist in Congress as for a parent choosing to volunteer one of his children's kidneys for the benefit of a sibling – is that there are certain characteristics (class, sex, family identity) such that people who share those characteristics are more likely to choose in the same way than others who do not.

Corresponding to the idea that the proxy "is able to express the choice that the incompetent would have made because of individualized, subjective knowledge of the incompetent" is the notion of the ascriptive representative acting as a transmitter of the inferred desires of the principal – the "substituted-judgment" doctrine. The important point here is that there is no assumption that the choice being made is the "correct" or "right" one. Thus in the *Seiferth* case, where a minor refused to undergo surgery for the repair of a cleft palate, a proxy acting as ascriptive representative could not allow such surgery even if he thought that it would be better for

4 A. Capron, "The Authority of Others to Decide about Biomedical Interventions with Incompetents," in *Who Speaks for the Child?*, eds. W. Gaylin, R. Macklin (Hastings-on-Hudson, N.Y.: The Hastings Center, 1982), 115–52.

the child.[5] To do so would be to act as an interest representative – a proxy who makes an "objectively reasonable choice that will...serve the incompetent's interests." This is what Capron calls the "best-interests" doctrine.

In actuality, of course, these doctrines seldom appear in a pure form. As Capron points out, the subjective nature of the substituted-judgment rule is hedged with objective limitations. Even if there is reason to believe a particular incompetent might have wanted to give away his estate, the court will assume that no reasonable person would want to do so. And, conversely, the "best interests" of a child are often defined in terms of the wishes of its parents.

The debate about the nature of representation in the political context reflects a normative conflict over the proper role of the representative. Ought a representative to act as those he represents wish or as the representative perceives their best interests? Is the representative to make use of his independent judgment or to act merely as a transmitter of the wishes of the represented? Is the representative a trustee exercising discretion on behalf of his clients or an agent faithfully carrying out the orders of his master? Is the representative to act *on* behalf of his principal, or *in* behalf?

These two polarities are associated with Edmund Burke and John Stuart Mill. Burke views representatives as trustees who are obliged to vote in the best interests of the nation as a whole, but who are not bound or obligated to those they represent. Indeed, Burke thought representatives need not even be chosen by those they represent.

If a part of the kingdom is being well governed, its interest secured, then it is represented whether or not it has the franchise; if it is not represented actually, then it can be said to be represented *virtually*. Virtual representation is that in which there is a communion of interests and a sympathy in feelings and desires between those who act in the name of any description of people, and the people in whose name they act, though the trustees are not actually chosen by them.[6]

Mill, on the other hand, was unequivocal that representatives

<hr>

5 See the discussion of this case in J. Goldstein, "Medical Care for the Child at Risk," in *Who Speaks for the Child?*, 153–88.

6 Edmund Burke, "The English Constitutional System," in Pitkin, *Representation*, 169–70.

must be chosen by those whom they represent, and, though somewhat ambivalent on this matter, thought that the representative should act as an agent of those he represents.

The meaning of representative government is that the whole people, or some numerous portion of them, exercise through deputies periodically elected by themselves the ultimate controlling power, which, in every constitution, must reside somewhere.[7]

It is clear from an examination of their works that Burke's and Mill's differing views of the proper role of the representative reflect very different views of human nature, of the capacities of the representative and the represented, of the nature of political issues. Compare, for example, the respective views of Burke and Mill on the question of whether the people know their own interests.

The most poor, illiterate, and uninformed creatures are judges of a *practical* oppression. It is a matter of feeling; and as such persons generally have felt most of it, and are not of an overlively sensibility, they are the best judges of it. But for *the real cause*, or *the appropriate remedy*, they ought never to be called into council about the one or the other. They ought to be totally shut out; because their reason is weak, because, when once roused, their passions are ungoverned; because they want information.[8]

Human beings are only secure from evil at the hands of others in proportion as they have the power of being, and are, self-protecting; and they only achieve a high degree of success in their struggle with Nature in proportion as they are self-dependent, relying on what they themselves can do, either separately or in concert, rather than on what others do for them.[9]

The issue of the "competence" of those who are being represented is perhaps the central question in the medical context with respect to proxy consent. But political theorists also differ concerning the nature of the decisions a representative makes, and this conflict is also reflected in their differences concerning the proper role of the representative.

As Pitkin puts it:

The more [a theorist] conceives of political issues as having correct, objectively determinable solutions accessible to rational inquiry, the more he will incline to independence [for the representative]; there is no point in

7 John Stuart Mill, "Considerations on Representative Government," in Pitkin, *Representation*, 180–1.
8 Burke, *English System*, 172.
9 Mill, *Representative Government*, 178.

counting noses accurately among the constituents if the question is a technical one calling for expertise. . . . The more political issues strike him as involving irrational commitment or personal preference, choice rather than deliberation, the more necessary it will seem that the representative consult the people's preferences and pursue their choice.[10]

This controversy occurs in the biomedical context as well. Goldstein's discussion of the *Sampson* case shows the judge's view of what determines a happy life (the absence of disfigurement) as an objective, rational matter – not to be impeded by an (irrational) person's preference.[11]

PROXY CONSENT

It is important to bear in mind two essential respects in which the political context differs from the biomedical. In the political area, some speak for others not (usually) because the others are incompetent but because – barring the special case of direct democracy (New England town meetings) – it is not feasible for all to make policy on a regular basis. The closest political analog to the issue of incompetence is the issue of colonial rule, which played a significant role in nineteenth-century political debate. Even Mill thought that colonial peoples were an exception to his view that each person is the best judge of his own interests, and he classified them with children as those in "non-age."

Related to this issue of the importance of incompetence is the second dis-analogy. Representatives are usually assumed to be chosen or authorized by those they represent. Representatives can act on behalf of others because they have been granted the right to do so. In the medical context, however, we have, because of "incompetence," a lack of explicit authorization. The dying patient in a coma, unless he has made a "living will" or otherwise expressed his intentions, has not designated a proxy to act on his behalf. The child has not chosen his parents as his representatives with the right to volunteer him for drug experiments. Whatever the merits of the mother's decision to choose abortion for a fetus, her right to do so does not derive from the consent of that fetus.

Thus in the medical context we have both "incompetence" and lack of specific authorization. How does this fact affect the question

10 Pitkin, *Representation*, 20–1.
11 J. Goldstein, *Who Speaks for the Child*, 180–3.

of what the proper role of the "proxy" ought to be? To begin with, it raises obvious moral issues having to do with the normal right of individuals to autonomy in the sense of self-determination. An agent is being denied the right to make certain decisions concerning his physical and emotional welfare. It is interesting to note that this situation does not always involve coercion or manipulation – the normal paths to deprivation of liberty.

It is the rare case, such as the refusal to allow a severe-burn victim to leave the hospital and die, that explicitly denies liberty. More usual is the denial of opportunity or power, as in the case of a doctor who refuses a minor the operation that will remove one of her kidneys and transfer it to a sibling.

It is clear how abrogation of the right of self-determination involves other values as well. Our self-esteem and sense of worth are bound up with the right to determine what shall be done to and with our bodies and minds. The obvious justification for some system of delegated authority in the case of those who are incompetent to make certain decisions is that they have already "lost" that right – rather than having had it taken away by others. And given that some decisions will have to be made, the only significant issues are who shall make them and what criteria should guide their judgment. Proxy consent does not serve the same purpose as "real" consent – to ensure that a person is only exposed to those medical interventions that he has chosen freely in an informed fashion. If we insisted on actual consent, then no risky procedures intended to benefit the child as patient could ever be performed. Because it seems contrary to the best interests of the child to adopt such a policy, we decide to accept the consent of a proxy, and choose the parents as the proxies.

The reasons for selecting parents reflects a number of different sociological, psychological, and administrative considerations. These include respect for the family as a decision-making unit; the appropriateness of giving the power of consent to those individuals who were responsible for bringing the child into the world, and who have a legal and moral duty to protect it; the belief that, of all the possible proxies, the parents are most likely to have the interests of the child foremost; and the belief that the administrative costs of assigning this function to other parties (an ombudsman) would be too high. Each of these considerations may be legitimately questioned on both empirical (the high incidence of battered children) and moral (the link between procreation and proprietary rights is dubious) grounds. But because it is extremely unlikely that we shall turn to other candidates for proxies, I prefer to concentrate on the question of the criteria that parents ought to use in choosing for their children. As unauthorized representatives, should they act as the child desires or would desire, or make an independent judgment of what is in the child's best interests?

In the medical context, as in the political, the answer is that neither is always the right thing to do. One needs to distinguish the following variables that affect the matter. In each case I shall give examples from both the medical and political realms.

What is the nature of the issue about which the decision is being made? In the political context one might want to pay more attention to the expressed wishes of one's constituents about an economic issue, say minimum-wage legislation, and less attention if the issue was one of infringing important civil liberties. In the medical context a quality-of-life decision for a minor might call for more respect for his expressed wishes than would a life-and-death issue.

Second, what is the nature of the persons who are being represented? A representative might act as an agent for relatively sophisticated voters who care about issues, and more as a trustee for relatively naive and unconcerned voters. In the medical context a crucial variable is the nature of the incompetence. A comatose adult is one who has attained competence at some point and then lost it. He, therefore, has had the opportunity to choose life plans, formulate desires and intentions, and so on. It will therefore be easier to infer what he would want were he not incompetent. Obviously, the duration of the incompetence also matters. What he would want, and what is in his interests, will differ depending on whether the incompetence is temporary or permanent.

In the case of children (or those who have been mentally incompetent since they were children) we are dealing with those who have never attained competence and therefore have not been able to choose life plans, form various intentions, develop certain desires, and so on. In such a case, if it is expected that competence will be attained at some point, we ought to choose for them, not as they might want, but in terms of maximizing those interests that will make it possible for them to develop life plans of their own. We ought to preserve their share of what John Rawls calls "primary goods"; that is, such goods as liberty, health, and opportunity,

which any rational person would want to pursue whatever particular life plan he chooses.

What are the interests at stake? A political representative may
have to balance the interests and desires of some against those of
others. He may have to consider the interests of current generations
against the needs or interests of future generations. This question
of balancing conflicts of interests occurs in the case of incompetents
as well. The case of Lausier v. Pescinski illustrates this fact dra-
matically.[12] A mother of six contracted glomerulonephritis, under-
went a total nephrectomy, and required a kidney transplant. Her
brother had been institutionalized for twenty of his thirty-eight
years as a "catatonic schizophrenic." Another sister, who was ap-
pointed the guardian for the brother, petitioned the court to approve
a transplant. The court denied permission, arguing:

> An incompetent particularly should have his own interests protected. Cer-
> tainly no advantage should be taken of him. In the absence of real consent
> on his part, and in a situation where no benefit to him has been established,
> we fail to find any authority for the county court or this court, to approve
> this operation.[13]

The lone dissenter argued in terms of what the incompetent would
have consented to as opposed to what was in his benefit. He con-
cluded that "in all probability" the brother would consent because
"for him it would be a short period of discomfort which would
not affect his ability either to enjoy life or his longevity."[14] Thus,
because the issue was one of a relatively small risk to the incompetent (it was estimated in testimony before the court to be comparable to the risk of driving) and life or death for the potential
donee, the dissenting judge was willing to use the doctrine of substituted judgment (what the incompetent would have done) as opposed to the best-interests test.

I would agree that such inferences are wholly without warrant
in the absence of any specific evidence about the incompetent's
attitude toward his sister, his inclinations to altruism, his attitude
toward risk, and so on. The proxy in such a case ought to be

12 Lausier v. Pescinski, 67 Wis. 2nd 4, 226 N.W. 2nd 180, 1975.
13 67 Wis. 2d at 8, 9 226 N.W. 2d at 182.
14 67 Wis. 2d at 12, 226 N.W. 2d at 183. For further discussion of this case and of
    the more general issue of the doctrine of substituted judgment see John R.
    Robertson, "Organ Donation by Incompetents and the Substituted Judgement
    Doctrine," *Columbia Law Review* 76 (1976), 48–78.

required, as the majority held, to act only in terms of the interests, objectively ascertained, of the incompetent.

Let me suggest, in conclusion, a set of problems that deserve intensive philosophical investigation because of their significance for the issue of proxy consent. The first is that of the interconnections between the concepts of interests and consent. It is normally assumed that people would choose what is in their interests; hence, arguments for inferring what people would choose will often make reference to their (perceived) interests. Conversely, our conception of what is in a person's interest is often a function of what he would choose. Thus it could be argued that the decision not to transfuse blood to a comatose Jehovah's Witness is a decision made in his interest (even though he will die as a result), because his interest is defined in terms of the choices he regards as morally appropriate. How, therefore, can we conceptually characterize these notions to exhibit both their differences and their interrelations?

Second, with respect to competent persons we normally believe that when their choices conflict with their interests (as others perceive them), their choice ought to be respected – in other words, the Millian antagonism to paternalism.[15] To what extent, then, ought this respect for choice be carried over to incompetents? If the person, when competent, would have made what we regard as a foolish decision, ought we make that decision for him when he is incompetent?

Finally, if we are going to depend on some notion of "hypothetical consent," what the incompetent would have chosen if, then what follows the if? Would have chosen, if competent? But that cannot always be what is meant. Consider the sterilization of the mentally retarded. There is a reasonable argument that a mentally retarded person would choose to be sterilized, since only by doing so would he be allowed to have a sex life. But, if we are considering how he would have chosen *if not mentally retarded*, then there would be no obstacle to his sexual activity, and no need to make such a

---

15 For some exceptions and objections to this doctrine, see my "Paternalism," reprinted in Gorovitz et al., *Moral Problems in Medicine* (Englewood Cliffs, N.J.: Prentice-Hall, 1976).

choice. Again, should "if he were to recover competence" follow? But he may never have had it. Should it be a matter of "if he were to attain competence"? But, if we know he never will, why should that be the appropriate condition? The most plausible candidate is "if he were competent but knew he would become incompetent in this particular fashion." In short, we need a careful examination of what is meant by "what the incompetent would choose," as well as a moral theory that indicates that the conditions we posit in such an analysis are the morally appropriate ones. In other words, we need a theory of what it is to respect an incompetent person as a person. Unfortunately, at this point, we lack such a theory for competent persons as well.[16]

16 I would like to thank Ruth Macklin and Leslie Dach for their helpful suggestions on an earlier draft.

7

Autonomy and informed consent

"Why do you assume you have the right to decide for someone else? Don't you agree it's a terrifying right, one that rarely leads to good? You should be careful. No one's entitled to it, not even doctors."

"But doctors *are* entitled to the right – doctors above all," exclaimed Dontsova with deep conviction. By now she was really angry. "Without that right there'd be no such thing as medicine!"

Solzhenitsyn, *Cancer Ward*

The slave doctor prescribes what mere experience suggests – and when he has given his orders, like a tyrant, he rushes off. But the other doctor, who is a freeman, attends and practices upon freemen – he enters into a discourse with the patient and with his friends – and he will not prescribe for him until he has first convinced him: at last, when he has brought the patient more and more under his persuasive influences and set him on the road to health, he attempts to effect a cure.

Plato, *The Laws*

In ethics, as in the law, there is often agreement concerning what to do in a particular case, or about the importance of a moral principle, co-existing with disagreement about why we should act in a certain manner, or on the nature or basis of the moral principle. Similarly, moral theories may agree about specific cases of lying while giving different accounts of why a lie is or is not justified. Becoming clearer about the sources of our principles or judgments is of both practical and theoretical importance. For agreement in particular judgments may conceal the possibility of disagreement in cases not yet encountered. Understanding the deeper sources of our judgments allows us to anticipate such divergences between ourselves and others. At the theoretical level, understanding the

This chapter was originally published in *Making Health Care Decisions*, vol. 3 (Washington, D.C.: U.S. Government Printing Office, 1982), 63–81. Reprinted by permission.

bases of our principles and judgments provides one mode of testing our moral theories. For the task of a theory is not to match our judgments but to account for those that are sound and criticize those that are faulty. A good theory unifies and explains its data and generates new judgments that are tested against our moral experience.

In this essay I shall consider the doctrine of informed consent, as it appears in the context of health care, and the various concepts that have been put forward as a basis for it. In particular I shall focus on the concept of autonomy, attempting to clarify its nature, distinguish it from other concepts, and defend its claim to be at the center of the justificatory basis for informed consent.

JUSTIFICATIONS FOR INFORMED CONSENT

It is clear from examination of the legal and philosophical literature on informed consent that its defense has involved appeals to very different kinds of considerations. I give here a sample of typical assertions of such claims. Many of them come from the legal, rather than philosophical, literature. This is natural because the doctrine is a creature of law. But my interest in the doctrine is as a moral, not, a legal view. I make this distinction, not because moral and legal contexts are sharply separated, but to remind the reader that the law has specific features (such as the need to make a decision) that do not allow one to argue directly from a legal justification to more general normative conclusions.

In our view, the patient's right of self-decision shapes the boundaries of the duty to reveal ... And to safeguard the patient's interest in achieving his own determination on treatment, the law must itself set the standard for adequate disclosure.[1]

The constitutional right of privacy includes the right of a mature competent adult to refuse to accept medical recommendations that may prolong one's life and which, to a third person at least, appear to be in his best interests.[2]

Anglo-American law starts with the premise of thorough-going self-determination. It follows that each man is considered to be master of his own body, and he may, if he be of sound mind, expressly prohibit the performance of lifesaving surgery.[3]

1 Canterbury v. Spence, 464 F.2d (D.C. Cir.) at 786.
2 In re Yetter, 62 Pa. D&C 2d 619 at 623.
3 Nathanson v. Kline, 186 Kan. 393 at 406.

The requirement of informed consent has two parts, both of which must be met before a medical intervention is permissible: first, that sufficient information be disclosed to the patient so that he can arrive at an intelligent opinion, and second, that the patient agrees to the intervention being performed. The latter facet in particular reflects the concern, traditional in western societies, that the autonomy of the person be respected . . . autonomy is centrally associated with the notion of individual responsibility. The freedom to make decisions for oneself carries with it the obligation to answer for the consequences of those decisions.[4]

The purpose of requiring the patient's consent to treatment is to protect his physical and psychic integrity against unwanted invasions, and to permit the patient to act as an autonomous, self-determining being.[5]

The very foundation of the doctrine (of informed consent) is every man's right to forego treatment or even cure if it entails what for him are intolerable consequences or risks, however warped or perverted his sense of values may be in the eyes of the medical profession, or even of the community, so long as any distortion falls short of what the law regards as incompetency. Individual freedom here is guaranteed only if people are given the right to make choices which would generally be regarded as foolish ones.[6]

The principle of an informed consent is a statement of the fidelity between the man who performs medical procedures and the man on whom they are performed . . . The principle of an informed consent is the canon of loyalty joining men together in medical practice and investigation.[7]

[T]here does seem to exist a positive right of informed consent which exists both in therapeutic and experimental settings . . . From whence derives this right? It arises from the right each of us possesses to be treated as a person.[8]

Although the requirement of informed consent is not traditional in Hippocratic medicine, it is possible to justify such a requirement on patient-benefitting grounds. Indeed, if we recognize that judgments about what is beneficial to a particular patient will vary from patient to patient depending upon the particular norms and values of that person, a strong case can be made that informing patients of treatment alternatives so that they

---

4 A. M. Capron, "Informed Consent in Catastrophic Disease Research & Treatment," *University of Pennsylvania Law Review* 123 (December 1974), 365.
5 A. Meisel, "The 'Exceptions' to the Informed Consent Doctrine: Striking a Balance Between Competing Values in Medical Decision-making," *Wisconsin Law Review* (1979, no. 2), 420.
6 F. Harper and F. James. *The Law of Torts* (Suppl 68), 61.
7 P. Ramsey, *The Patient as Person* (New Haven: Yale University Press, 1970), 5.
8 B. Freeman, "A Moral Theory of Consent," *Hastings Center Report* (August 1975), 32.

can participate in or even control the decision-making process will increase the likelihood that patient-benefits will be maximized.[9]

I have not listed a class of justification that also appears in the literature. In these an appeal is made to the good consequences for others that would follow from adhering to the doctrine of informed consent. This functional analysis, exemplified by the work of Jay Katz, relies on the encouragement of rational decision making, the protection of the experimental process, increasing society's awareness of the research process, and so forth. I am not denying that such reasons can play a part in the justification of informed consent but I wish to focus on defenses that refer to some property of the individual whose consent is being sought, because I believe, but will not argue here, these operate at a more fundamental level than the appeal to more general consequences.

AUTONOMY, PRIVACY, AND LIBERTY: DISTINCTIONS

Our brief survey shows that informed consent is justified in terms of privacy, self-determination, loyalty, autonomy, freedom, integrity, dignity, and benefits. Individuals have the right to be treated as persons, as masters of their own body, as responsible for their decisions, as makers of choices. Though frequently these are regarded as equivalent notions it should be fairly obvious that they are quite different values.

Privacy and autonomy. To take the most glaring case, consider the values of privacy and autonomy. Privacy consists of the ability of an individual to maintain control of the information about himself that is available to others. It is intimately linked with the idea of being scrutinized by others, although, with the invention of various devices for intercepting communications, it extends to what we say, think, or do. Thus, typical interferences with privacy include observations of our bodies, behavior, and interactions with others. The more control we have over knowledge about ourselves, the more privacy we maintain.

Without going into the analysis of autonomy I shall present be-

9 R. Veatch, "Three Theories of Informed Consent: Philosophical Foundations and Policy Implications," *The Belmont Report* (DHEW Publication No. OS 78–0014, 1982), 26–8.

low, it is clear that although privacy may be related to autonomy in a number of ways it is not identical with it. The relationship between the two concepts may be empirical: that is, it may be claimed that a condition for the development of our autonomy includes considerable respect for our privacy. The relationship may be conceptual: that is, it may be argued that to deny people privacy is to deny them the respect for personhood that is closely linked with their autonomy.

But a few examples should show that the concepts are distinct. One way of interfering with your autonomy is to deceive you. This interference with information is, however, just the opposite kind from that involved in interference with privacy. What is controlled is the information coming to you, not the information coming from you. I do not know something about you that you might wish to conceal. I conceal something from you that you might wish to know. Thus, autonomy but not privacy is diminished.

Similarly, privacy may be interfered with but not autonomy. If someone taps your phone conversations without your knowledge he interferes with your privacy. But your decisions, your actions, your values, are in no way changed or altered from what they might be otherwise. You are as self-determining as ever.

The intellectual disorder that arises from confusing these two notions may be observed in the Supreme Court decision in Griswold v. Connecticut that ruled that prohibition of the use of contraceptives was a violation of the constitutional right of privacy. Whatever the misdeeds of the state of Connecticut in this matter it did not involve any attempt to get acquainted with the personal lives of its citizens. It did involve attempting to interfere with the procreative decisions of citizens, and hence raised issues of autonomy and liberty – but these are quite different issues. One reason for the confusion of the concepts is that violations of autonomy and of privacy exhibit a common failure to respect another person as an independent moral agent. But they do so in different ways and ought not to be assimilated. In particular the doctrine of informed consent cannot rest on a notion of privacy. For it is the information flow to the patient that is at issue, not the patient's control over information about himself.

Liberty and autonomy. Whereas the distinction between autonomy and privacy is clear, the identification of liberty and autonomy is much more plausible and tempting. In this section I will argue that the two notions ought to be distinguished and the concept that most effectively grounds the doctrine of informed consent is autonomy.

I suggest we think of liberty (or freedom, which I use as a synonym) as the ability of a person to do what he wishes and to have significant options that are not closed or made less eligible by the actions of other agents or the workings of social institutions. Historically there have been two influential traditions that have explicated the idea of liberty in contrasting terms. On one view, associated with the names of Thomas Hobbes and John Stuart Mill, liberty is the absence of interference with a person's actions. Coercion and force are the main enemies of liberty. Another tradition, that of Jean Jacques Rousseau and T. H. Green, understands liberty as being more than simply the absence of interference, as including the presence of a range of alternatives and opportunities. But whether the emphasis is on restrictions or opportunities the core notion of liberty is the ability of a person to effectuate his decisions in action.

If, for example, a doctor forces a Jehovah's Witness to have a blood transfusion against his will, this is a direct interference with the liberty of the patient. But because this is also clearly a denial of the patient's autonomy, understood as a power of self-determination, the thought arises that autonomy and liberty are the same.

An example from John Locke shows us that they are not. Consider a person who is put into a prison cell and told that all the doors are locked. The guards go through the motion of locking the doors but in fact one of the locks is defective and the prisoner could simply open the door and leave the cell. Because he is not aware of this he, quite reasonably, remains in his cell. The prisoner is, in fact, free to leave the cell. His liberty has not, although he does not know this, been limited. His autonomy has been limited. His view of the alternatives open to him has been manipulated by the guards in such a fashion that he will not choose to leave. This example shows that self-determination can be limited without limiting liberty.

It might be suggested that although we can interfere with autonomy but not liberty, the converse does not hold; that all interference with liberty is necessarily interference with autonomy. For if we prevent a person from doing what he wishes, do we not interfere with the ability of a person to choose what he shall do, to fashion his life? Although this seems plausible I believe it is false. We accept the claim because we are used to focusing on cases where a person wishes to be free from interference, resents having his liberty taken away. Consider, however, the classical case of Odysseus.

Not wanting to be lured onto the rocks by the siren, Odysseus commands his men to tie him to the mast and refuse all later orders he might give to be set free. He wants to have his liberty limited so that he and his men will survive. Although his behavior at the time he hears the sirens is not free – he struggles against his bonds and orders his men to free him – there is another aspect of his conduct that must be understood if we are to evaluate his situation correctly. He has a preference about his preferences, a desire not to act upon certain desires. He views the desire to steer his ship toward the sirens, and the rocks, as an alien desire. In limiting his liberty in accordance with his wishes we promote, not hinder, his efforts to define the contours of his life. We promote his autonomy by denying him liberty.

Liberty is a concept that applies to the desires and preferences a person has for particular states of affairs. It focuses on what a person wants to do at the level of action. But this level ignores a crucial feature of persons – their capacity to reflect upon and adopt attitudes toward their desires, wishes, and values. It also ignores the ways that their desires and preferences were acquired. If it matters to persons not only what they value and believe but also the process by which they came to these states then only a fuller appreciation of their higher-order preferences will illuminate self-determination.

If one looks at the structure of the arguments for and against informed consent one has a better explanation of that structure by assuming that autonomy, not liberty, is the central value in the doctor–patient relationship. If we consider the main argument for denying the necessity of informed consent, that of therapeutic privilege, we see that this is a paternalistic argument. It is grounded on the idea that we ought to advance the patient's welfare even if this involves denying him the knowledge needed to make consent informed.

Attempts to define the concept of paternalism in the medical context view paternalism as the denial of liberty. One philosopher characterizes paternalism as "interference with a person's freedom of action or freedom of information, or the deliberate dissemination of misinformation."[10]

This definition implies that if a doctor does not misinform or fail to reveal information to a patient but tells the patient more than he wants to know the doctor does not act in a paternalistic fashion. But when a doctor insists upon telling a patient what he does not want to know, for his own good, this is a clear case of paternalism.

Or to consider a different kind of case, a husband might hide his sleeping pills fearing his wife's suicidal tendencies; again an act of paternalism, but not one that interferes with either freedom or the flow of information.

Only if one views paternalism as the denial of autonomy, as the substitution of one person's judgment for another, do these cases become paternalistic. The doctor who tells the patient more than he wants to know and the husband who hides the pills both substitute their judgment for another person's. There is a usurpation of decision making. I am not, at this point, arguing this is right or wrong. I am only claiming that if autonomy is the value against which paternalism offends we have an explanation of why certain acts are paternalistic – an explanation that is lacking in the view that it is liberty that is at stake.

Autonomy is a richer notion than liberty, which is conceived either as mere absence of interference or as the presence of alternatives. It is tied up with the idea of being a subject, of being more than a passive spectator of one's desires and feelings. Some of the flavor of this idea is presented by Isaiah Berlin.

I wish my life and decision to depend on myself, not on external forces of whatever kind. I wish to be the instrument of my own, not of other men's acts of will. I wish to be a subject, not an object; to be moved by reasons, by conscious purposes, which are my own, not by causes which affect me, as it were, from outside. I wish to be somebody, not anybody; a doer – deciding not being decided for, self-directed and not acted upon by external nature or by other men . . . I wish, above all, to be conscious of myself as a thinking, willing, active being, bearing responsibility for his choices and able to explain them by reference to his own ideas and purposes.[11]

10 A. Buchanan, "Medical Paternalism," *Philosophy and Public Affairs* 7 (Summer 1978), 372.
11 I. Berlin, *Two Concepts of Liberty* (Oxford: Clarendon Press, 1969), 123.

It is this notion that I want to develop more carefully and that provides the soundest basis for explaining and justifying the doctrine of informed consent.

The concept of autonomy. The central idea that underlies the concept of autonomy is indicated by the etymology of the term: *autos* (self) and *nomos* (rule or law). The term was first applied to the Greek city state. A city had *autonomia* when its citizens made their own laws, as opposed to being under the control of some conquering power. There is then a natural extension to persons as being autonomous when their decisions and actions are their own.

It is characteristic of persons, and seems to be a distinctively human ability, that they are able to reflect upon and adopt attitudes towards their desires, intentions, life plans. One may not just desire to smoke but also desire that one not have that desire. One may be motivated by jealousy and anger and also desire that one's motivations be different.

A person may identify with the influences that motivate him, view himself as the kind of person who wishes to be moved in particular ways. Or he may resent being motivated in certain ways, be alienated from those influences, prefer to be the kind of person who has different values and preferences. I am defining autonomy as the capacity to reflect upon one's motivational structure and to make changes in that structure. Thus, autonomy is not simply a reflective capacity but also includes some ability to alter one's preferences and to make them effective in action. Indeed to make them effective partly because one has reflected upon them and adopted them as one's own.

Autonomy is a second-order capacity to reflect critically upon one's first-order preferences and desires, and the ability either to identify with these or to change them in light of higher-order preferences and values. By exercising such a capacity we define our nature, give meaning and coherence to our lives, and take responsibility for the kind of person we are.

Liberty, power, and privacy are not equivalent to autonomy but they may be necessary conditions for individuals to develop their own aims and interests, and to make their values effective in the living of their lives.

It is an implication of my view that there is no specific content to the decisions an autonomous person takes. Someone who wishes to be the kind of person who does whatever the doctor orders is as autonomous as the person who wants to evaluate those orders for himself. This view differs from others in the literature. R. P. Wolff, for example, says (in the context of the citizen and the state) "[t]he autonomous man . . . may do what another tells him, but not because he has been told to do it . . . By accepting as final the commands of the others he forfeits his autonomy."[12] But this conception of autonomy not only has the consequence that no government is legitimate but also that such values as loyalty, objectivity, commitment, and love are inconsistent with being autonomous.

Although I do not believe there is a direct logical link between acting autonomously and being critical and independent in judging and acting, it is plausible to suppose there are psychological connections. It is likely that those who practice in their life a critical reflection on their values will tend to be suspicious of modes of thought that rely on the uncritical acceptance of authority, tradition, and custom.

It should also not be thought that those who autonomously choose to follow the commands of others can thereby escape responsibility for their actions. A person is responsible for ceding his independence to another. What does affect responsibility is interference with a person's autonomy when the person is not in a position to realize this is occurring, or to do much about it if he does. If my will is overborne or undermined, then the responsibility for what I have done shifts to those who have interfered with my autonomy.

THE VALUE OF AUTONOMY IN INFORMED CONSENT

I have argued so far that the concept of autonomy plays a major role in arguments about the requirement of informed consent but I have not yet said very much about why the promotion of autonomy is something to be desired and valued. This question is made more difficult by the particular conception of autonomy I have presented. For a conception of autonomy that has no particular content, that allows for the possibility of a patient granting complete authority to a doctor, seems too formal to be of great value. I shall argue now that it is precisely because autonomy has this relatively

12 R. P. Wolff, *In Defense of Anarchism* (New York: Harper & Row, 1970), 14.

weak and formal character that it can play a fundamental role in moral theory.

Let me begin by considering at the most general level what is involved in that form of practical reasoning we single out as moral reasoning. Every moral theory has some conception of equality among moral agents, some conception according to which we are to regard others as equal to ourselves. For the utilitarian, equality is represented in the theory by the claim that in calculating utility the interests of each person are to count equally. For the natural rights theorist, all persons are assumed to have equal rights. For the Kantian, I may act only in that way that I am prepared to will all others act. For the religious moralist we are all children of God.

Corresponding to these notions of equality are various devices for preserving this fundamental equality in the process of moral reasoning. According to the utilitarian an action is justified when an impartial observer would view the action as maximizing the total amount of utility in the given community. For the rights theorist and the Kantian a justification must be acceptable to each of the individuals affected. A similar motive underlies the Golden Rule that is found in most major religious theories.

Underlying the various techniques of moral justification is a prohibition against treating others in such a way that they cannot share the purposes of those who are so treating them. And behind this is a conception of the nature of persons as independent sources of moral agency. It is as distinct loci of consciousness, of purposive action, as distinct selves, that others must be respected and taken into account when each of us decides what he shall do. It is because other persons are creators of their own lives, are shapers of their own values, are the originators of projects and plans, that their interests must be taken into account, their rights respected, their projects valued.

What makes an individual the particular person he is reflects his pursuit of autonomy, his construction of meaning in his life. One can see, therefore, a number of reasons why autonomy is a relatively contentless notion. People can give meaning to their lives in innumerable ways. There is no particular way of giving shape or meaning to a life. This, of course, is compatible with certain lives being more admirable than others. In addition, any feature that is going to ground an equality of respect must be a feature that persons share, that they have in common. Any particular way of filling in the content of a life plan is not likely to be shared. Morality is owed to everyone. More intimate relationships such as friend or lover must respond to the particular qualities of another, to lives shaped in specific fashion. Moral respect is owed to all because all have (assuming we are dealing with normal persons, not defective or incompetent in serious ways) the capacity for autonomous development.

Now it is true that although all (normal) persons have such a capacity it is not the case that all have an equal capacity. Like any other capacity – say, the ability to identify with the pain of others – it is a product of one's biological and environmental circumstances. Our conception of a moral agent is of a creature who possesses this capacity above some significant threshold. That some persons will be very much above this level is not important, morally speaking, although it may be important for some purposes.

This first part of my argument has been directed to showing that a weak notion of autonomy is connected to central parts of ethical reasoning. It is also linked to important metaphysical and attitudinal features of moral agents. Our idea of who we are, of our self-identity, is linked to our ability to find and refine ourselves. The exercise of the capacity of autonomy is what makes my life *mine*. And, if I am to recognize others as equal persons, there is a requirement that I give weight to the way they define and value the world in deciding how I should act.

One argument, then, for the value of autonomy is that we have a conception of persons that is deeply rooted in our world view, and that this conception is worthy of respect and admiration. A full analysis of why the capacity for autonomy is worthy of respect would require a general theory of value (worth) and of morality (respect). I have neither but I shall make some comments about the value of autonomy.

Arguments for the value of anything may claim that something is good because it leads to something else that is good (instrumental value) or because it is good for its own sake (intrinsic value). Autonomy has value along both dimensions.

On instrumental grounds, being able to shape one's own choices and values makes it more likely that one's life will be satisfying than if others, even benevolent others, do the shaping. This is the

111

traditional liberal argument that people are better judges of their own interests than others. Though debate goes on about the limits to which this is true, as a rough generalization it is highly probable.

There is also the fact that quite aside from what results from determining one's life, people get satisfaction out of doing so. We should not overlook the extent to which the process of thinking about, reflecting upon, choosing among preferences is a source of satisfaction to individuals.

But there is value connected with being self-determining that is not a matter either of bringing about good results or the pleasures of the process itself. This is the intrinsic desirability of exercising the capacity for self-determination. We desire to be recognized by others as the kind of creature capable of determining our own destiny. Our own sense of self-respect is tied to the respect of others – and this is not just a matter of psychology. Second, notions of creativity, of risk-taking, of adherence to principle, of responsibility are all linked conceptually to the possibility of autonomous action. These desirable features of a good life are not possible (logically) for nonautonomous creatures. In general, autonomy is linked to activity, to making rather than being, to those higher forms of consciousness that are distinctive of human potential.

It should not be denied that in addition to the instrumental gains of exercising autonomy there are also instrumental losses. With responsibility comes blame and punishment. With the possibility of adherence to principle comes the possibility of cowardice and betrayal. It is not part of my thesis that more autonomy is always better than less. I have only been trying to understand why autonomy has value when it does.

THE SPECIAL ROLE OF AUTONOMY IN HEALTH CARE

I turn now to the question of whether autonomy plays some special role in the health-care context. We know that there are various professional relationships that attach significance to the autonomy of the client. A psychiatrist may point out the destructive aspects of a marriage but ought not to pressure his patient to terminate it. Architects must walk the fine line between respecting the wishes of the client and attempting to educate and refine his taste in houses. Is autonomy more important in the doctor–patient relationship than

112

in these other cases? I believe there is something special about the health-care context that emerges from an accurate conception of the doctor's role.

It is a truism that a doctor cares for the health of the body. It is also a truism that persons are embodied creatures; meaning not merely that we have bodies but that we are bodies. From these truisms it follows that the care of our bodies is linked with our identity as persons. Whatever goals or values we have are tied up with the fate of our bodies. Health is, as John Rawls puts it, a primary good, a good that any person wishes to preserve and promote whatever the more specific details of his life plans. The function of medical care has been put most succinctly by Charles Fried.

[T]he doctor's prime and basic function is not so much the prevention of death (which is not in his power) but the preservation of life capacities for the realization of a reasonable, realistic life plan. As in particular cases conflicts arise and decisions must be made between various capacities and between the risk of death and the impairment of various capacities, the doctor must see himself as the servant, not of life in the abstract, but of life plans of his patients.[13]

Decisions about what form of treatment to undergo, the probabilities of cure and of side effects, judgments about how the body will look to others after various forms of surgery, whether to spend one's last days in a hospital or at home – these are not technical, medical judgments. To suppose that these are matters of expertise, decisions to be taken by experts, represents a denial of autonomy that is particularly damaging for two reasons.

First, one's body is irreplaceable and inescapable. If my architect doesn't listen to me and this results in a house I do not like, I can always move. I cannot move from my body. In addition because my body *is* me, failure to respect my wishes concerning my body is a particularly insulting denial of autonomy. Of course the opposite side of this coin is also true. If the denial of autonomy is justified in terms of promoting the benefit of my body then paternalism would seem to have the strongest claim in the medical context. This brings us to the issue of possible exceptions to respecting the autonomy of patients.

13 C. Fried, *Medical Experimentation: Personal Integrity and Social Policy* (New York: Elsevier, 1974), 98.

Thus far I have argued that autonomy plays a major role in explaining the doctrine of informed consent and I have given reasons for the importance we attach to autonomy. But nothing I have said commits me to the view that respect for autonomy is, or ought to be, absolute. There are certainly other values that are of fundamental moral importance and of crucial significance to any person. These include dignity, health, well-being, integrity, security. It is possible that in order to promote any of these values it may be necessary to sacrifice some autonomy. It is also possible that promotion of autonomy in the long run requires sacrificing autonomy in the short run. Finally there are cases in which a person is already in a non-autonomous state or one of diminished autonomy and the principle ceases to have application or at least its application is more problematic than in normal cases. These seem to me the grounds for considering exceptions to the doctrine of informed consent – conflicting values and reduced autonomy – and I want to indicate the framework of moral justification that I think is appropriate for discussing the limits to principles we judge to be, at first approximation, the correct ones. I shall not argue for this framework – indeed it is not clear that such a basic outlook can be argued for – but simply present it in the hope that it will strike the reader as plausible and attractive.

Moral reasoning is a branch of practical reasoning, that is, reasoning about what to do as opposed to how things are. Unlike other kinds of practical reasoning, for example, prudential thought about what will promote my long-range welfare, it is tied to the existence and recognition of other persons. Just as prudential reasoning is constrained by the recognition that there is a future self whose interests must be taken into account, moral reasoning is constrained by the recognition that there are other persons whose interests are no less important to them than mine are to me. Moral reasoning is the attempt to give reasons for action that are acceptable to other independent and equal moral agents. We seek general principles for the regulation of behavior that are such that they can command the agreement of other informed, rational, and free agents. The test of a proposed principle or action is that it would be found acceptable not just to the person who proposes it but to all those whom the action affects. Justification is *to* others; moral motivation, the connection of morality with our will, is supplied not by sympathy alone but by our need to act in such a fashion that our actions are both understandable to ourselves and acceptable to others.

This view is a species of meta-ethical theory traditionally labeled as contractualist. It is a meta-ethical view because it says nothing directly about the content of the moral principles that are justified contractually. It is possible that the principles that are capable of being agreed to will be similar to those of utilitarians or Kantians or natural law theorists. But it is the agreement to the principles that grounds them and not the reasons for the agreement. Whatever its other merits on purely philosophical grounds, such a contractualist scheme of justification is particularly appropriate for our problem – the exceptions to the doctrine of informed consent. On this view the exceptions must be capable of being justified to those whose consent will not be sought or honored. Naturally, to present this justification in the very context in which the issue arises would be self-defeating. If, for example, one believes that presenting a patient with the true facts of his diagnosis would be psychologically damaging one could hardly justify this failure to inform by stating to the patient that he would be harmed by telling him the truth of his condition. The justification, if there is one, must lie in a general agreement that is *ex ante*, which occurs or could occur before we are faced with the situation to which the exception applies. We have to deliberate about and agree upon the merits of exceptions to a principle (whether there are any and how broad they should be) in abstraction from the particular set of facts. This is not to say, of course, that a doctor faced with a real case is barred from thinking about the issue. It is to say that his thought ought to reflect, in the logic and the range of considerations he considers relevant, the position of persons who are to settle upon rules prior to their being faced with specific moral conflicts.

EXCEPTIONS TO THE REQUIREMENT OF INFORMED CONSENT

The candidates for exceptions to informed consent can be grouped under the headings of emergency, incompetence, waiver, and therapeutic privilege.[14] The first two are relatively unproblematic in principle although they may pose problems in practice of determining when they apply. Waiver is, I shall argue, not an infringement of autonomy at all. Therapeutic privilege is the exception that most directly infringes autonomy and raises the greatest problem for justifying an exception.

It is surely rational for autonomous persons to agree that life-saving treatment may be rendered without the consent of the patient in "emergency" situations. An emergency situation is one in which the patient is unable to give consent or to receive information. If a patient should object to this treatment afterward there is a clear justification that can be presented to him. "I acted to preserve your possibility of future autonomous action," says the doctor, "and I did so in conditions such that you could not give your consent, and in which to wait until you could would be impossible."

Note here that it is not just that important benefits for the patient are produced but that there is no reason to suppose the patient did not want the benefits *and* there was no possibility of getting consent. We have a great benefit (life) secured without any loss of autonomy. For us not to agree to such a bargain is irrational.

The possibility of broadening the concept of an emergency then arises. Suppose that it is not life but, say, limb that is at stake and consent is not impossible but costly (where cost might be defined in terms of the time necessary to get agreement). Let us suppose we have a person with a detached hand that could be reattached by immediate microsurgery. And let us suppose that the person only speaks Serbo-Croatian and the time necessary to get a translator would make the operation ineffective. Again the *ex ante* justification seems clear. Our interest in our limbs is an important one; the violation of autonomy, while greater than in the previous case (because it is possible to get consent), is minor.

Proceeding in this manner – by varying the nature of the harm to be averted as well as the costs of obtaining informed consent – we should be able to get a fix on the limits of the emergency exception. It seems plausible, for example, that there will be cases where we will insist upon consent but not upon full information (which is time-consuming and which may not be effective in con-

14 I am indebted to Meisel, op. cit., for his classification of the exceptions to informed consent.

ditions of great stress and pain). I do not insist that this scheme will give unique solutions. There may be hypothetical cases in which reasonable people will disagree about what rule they would agree to in advance of an emergency. Those may be precisely the cases that we leave to other institutions, such as courts, to decide on a case-by-case basis after the fact.

It is sometimes said of emergency cases that the patient has "implicitly" or "tacitly" agreed to the treatment, and hence there is no violation of autonomy. This way of talking is misleading. It suggests that there is really some consent that has taken place but one just has to know where to look for it. In fact, neither explicitly nor implicitly has any agreement taken place; if there is no loss of autonomy in these situations by not getting consent it is because autonomy has already been lost and not because the patient has really consented. My argument does not rely on any supposed agreement but on a set of principles that are justified because they are capable of securing agreement by rational agents under certain circumstances.

In the typical emergency situation, where the patient is unconscious and cannot give consent, the patient is also incompetent. The case of a psychotic patient or a senile patient or an infant are also cases where consent is impossible but here it is not a temporary problem. Again, on the level of theory, the situation does not seem too difficult. Here the problems are ones of definition, of drawing the line, of determining who ought to be authorized to consent for the patient, and what criteria should that authorized subject use. The theoretical justification is identical to the emergency case. Given that we all know we are subject to various incompetencies and that decisions may have to be made with great impact on our life chances, it is reasonable for us to "insure" against loss by authorizing health care when we are not able to do so. The case of incompetency is one in which our autonomy has already been impaired, lost, or not developed so there is no denial of autonomy on the part of the doctor. It is true there are other harms that may be inflicted on us. We may be kept alive in conditions that are insults to our dignity or privacy, and once aware of this we may want to establish limits to the treatment that is permissible without our explicit consent. But to deny any exception to the securing of informed consent, even in cases where we are not competent, would be self-defeating.

117

The next exception, that of waiver, is conceptually quite a distinct category. Like self-defense in the law, it ought to be considered a justification, not an excuse. It is not like the previous cases of emergency or incompetence in that one fails to get informed consent; it is that one ought not to try. If a patient has knowingly and freely requested of the doctor that he not be informed or consulted about his course of treatment then to seek to obtain informed consent would itself be a violation of autonomy. Again the difficulty is a practical one – determining that the waiver is not simply psychological denial or a process of infantilization or of giving in to the pressures of the doctor. Leaving these difficult problems aside, as I argued earlier, autonomy includes the possibility of a decision to give up one's independent determination about what one should do. While this decision may be foolish or unwise it can hardly be interfered with on the grounds of autonomy. If one denies the legitimacy of waiver this will be on the grounds that it is better for the patient not to act in this manner. And this brings us to the issue of paternalism and the last category – therapeutic privilege.

Therapeutic privilege may be conceived as the opposite side of the coin of waiver. In waiver the patient decides that certain information will be harmful or cause distress and that he would be better off not having it. In therapeutic privilege the doctor decides that securing informed consent would be harmful to the patient and that he is better off not having it. It is a privilege because it allows exemption from a duty; it is therapeutic because it is intended for the benefit of the patient. This exception raises the clearest conflict between the value of autonomy and what is considered the best interests of the patient.

Using the framework of seeking general agreement by all the relevant parties, the issue becomes what powers to ignore our consent can we agree to grant health professionals when they claim that seeking such consent would be harmful to us. It is useful to consider a spectrum of positions ranging from weak to strong powers.

The weakest position is that autonomy may be denied only in the interests of the autonomy of the patient. This exception would allow a doctor to withhold information only when a special harm would (be likely to) follow from the disclosure of information, namely, that harm that would result in the patient's being unable or being less able to make an autonomous decision about his treat-

118

ment. This justification is invoked in Canterbury v. Spence, when the court claimed the failure to disclose was justified because "it is recognized that patients occasionally become so ill or emotionally distraught on disclosure as to foreclose a rational decision."[15] Such an exception is maximally coherent with the principle of informed consent because it claims that the disclosure would in fact undercut the worth of the consent. Of course the fact that a doctor claims this harm would occur does not make it true, and there remains the problem of designing institutions to make the ratio of true claims as high as possible and to provide remedies for those denied their autonomy when the claim is unwarranted by the available evidence. Nevertheless this exception seems to be one we can all accept because it is justified in terms of the promotion of the value fostered by the principle to which it is an exception.

There is the much broader version of harm invoked by therapeutic privilege that is also present in another line of reasoning in Canterbury. On this view failure to disclose was justified because "risk disclosure poses such a threat of detriment to the patient as to become unfeasible or contraindicated from a medical point of view."[15] Here one can distinguish two ways in which such information might be contraindicated. In one case the disclosure has a direct harmful effect on the emotional state of the patient. He is distraught when he learns he has cancer or Hodgkin's disease. In the other kind of case the harm operates primarily via its effect on the treatment decision made by the patient. The doctor believes that disclosure would lead the patient to choose a form of treatment that is not optimal or perhaps even detrimental. Note that this is not equivalent to asserting the patient cannot make a rational or autonomous decision; it is a claim that the decision is wrong or mistaken.

What would be the results of allowing doctors to have the power to deny our autonomy when they believe that harm in one of these two forms would result? According to the mode of justification that I have been using, such powers must be publicly recognized and acknowledged. Granting such authority to doctors must undermine the atmosphere of trust between doctor and patient, for the doctor could not for long simply remain silent but would have to mislead and, in many cases, lie. We would all be in a state of

15 Canterbury v. Spence, at 789.

uncertainty about the meaning and truth of the communications from doctor to patient.

Given the possibility of explicit waiver, given the state of dependency to which illness reduces us in any case, given the erosion of trust produced by such an exception, and given the difficulty of effective restraints on the use of such powers, the resulting loss of autonomy created by the wide exception of therapeutic privilege is too great to secure general agreement among all those concerned. Competent patients have the right to the information necessary to make those evaluative, nontechnical decisions about their bodies that autonomy requires.

Let me end by mentioning one final distinction. One may view the requirement of informed consent as connected to autonomy in either of two ways. In the first it is related as cause and effect. We suppose the requirement is, as a matter of fact, likely to promote the autonomy of patients. I believe the evidence is in favor of this proposition but it is an empirical claim subject to refutation. There is another way of viewing the connection, which sees the attempts to secure consent as itself being an expression of respect for the autonomy of the patient. On this view the connection is a necessary one. One way of showing respect for a person is by seeking his willing acceptance of a plan of treatment. Seeking consent is an expression of respect for autonomy in the way that apology is an expression of regret. To fail to seek consent, as in the case of therapeutic privilege, is necessarily an insult to autonomy even though motivated by pure benevolence.

8

Paternalism:
some second thoughts

"I changed my mind."
"Oh, yeah? Does it work any better?"
From a Mae West movie

I

As seems appropriate for second thoughts, I shall begin at the beginning—the definition of paternalism. Elsewhere, I defined the concept as "interference with a person's liberty of action justified by reasons referring exclusively to the welfare, good, happiness, needs, interests, or values of the person being coerced."[1]

A number of critics have objected that confining the concept to interference with liberty is too restrictive in scope.[2] Given the problem I was interested in, that is, the proper limits of state coercion, this restriction was reasonable, although even here one ought to be aware that the state has other ways of influencing people's behavior. It may refuse to enforce contracts, give in-kind rather than cash aid, set up licensing boards, require manufacturers to install seatbelts as original equipment, and so forth.

If, however, one wishes to consider the issue of paternalism in other contexts, for example, in the professions, one will need a broader definition. Not all paternalistic acts are acts of the state. Not all paternalistic acts involve interference with liberty. The doctor who lies to her terminally ill patients, the parent who stipulates in her will that a child may not inherit an estate before the age of thirty, the psychiatrist who tells his adolescent patient that he must

This chapter was originally published in *Paternalism*, ed. R. Sartorius (Minneapolis: University of Minnesota Press, 1983), 105–11. Reprinted by permission.
1 Gerald Dworkin, "Paternalism," *The Monist* 56 (January 1972), p. 65.
2 See, for example, Bernard Gert and Charles Culver, "Paternalistic Behavior," *Philosophy and Public Affairs* 6 (Fall 1976), 45–57.

121

inform her parents of her drug use, the professor who refuses to recommend her Ph.D. student to a certain university because he will be "out of his league" – these are all cases of paternalism that do not involve the use of coercion or force and, therefore, on standard views of liberty do not involve restrictions on liberty.

How should one broaden the definition? One way is to include such specific elements as deception. Allen Buchanan, for example, characterizes paternalism as "interference with a person's freedom of action or freedom of information, or the deliberate dissemination of misinformation."[3]

Given a suitably broad notion of freedom of information, this definition will include not only the case of a doctor acting paternalistically toward a patient by misinforming him or by not revealing information, but also the case of a doctor telling the patient more than he wants to know. A patient may make it quite clear that he does not want to know something about his condition and a doctor may insist on telling him the whole truth for his own good.

Still this definition seems too restrictive in scope. There are other ways to paternalize besides coercing or manipulating one's information set. Suppose, for example, we play tennis together and I realize that you are getting upset about the frequency with which you lose to me. So, for your own good and against your wishes, I refuse to play with you. My refusal to engage in a form of social cooperation does not seem to me an infringement of your liberty. But it also seems to me a case of paternalism.

On the other hand, the attempt to broaden the notion by including any violation of a moral rule is too restrictive because it will not cover cases such as the following.[4] A husband who knows his wife is suicidal hides his sleeping pills. He violates no moral rule. They are his pills and he can put them wherever he wishes.

This example, as well as that of the doctor who tells the patient the truth against his wishes, also works against defining paternalism in terms of acts that violate the rights of the person in question. The wife does not have a right to those pills, nor does the patient have a right not to be told the truth.

---

3 Allen Buchanan, "Medical Paternalism," *Philosophy and Public Affairs* 7 (Summer, 1978), 372.
4 This condition is Gert and Culver's.

It begins to look as if the only condition that will work is one that depends upon the fact that the person who is being treated paternalistically does not wish to be treated that way. The wife has no right to the pills, but she does not want her husband to hide them. The patient has no right to not be told the truth, but he doesn't want to hear it. But something more must be present in order to include a case like the following.

Consider a father (a lawyer) who wants his daughter to become a lawyer. The daughter believes that she would make a very good lawyer. Indeed, she believes it likely that she would be more successful professionally than her father, who has managed to survive only on a marginal basis. Because she believes that such success would make her father very unhappy, the daughter decides to become a doctor instead. Here is a decision made against the wishes of another person for that person's own good. Yet, I think that this is not a case of paternalism. The daughter does nothing to interfere with the self-determination of the father. She does not act in accordance with her father's judgment, but neither does she act in such a fashion as to substitute her judgment for that of her father.

There must be a violation of a person's autonomy (which I conceive as a distinct notion from that of liberty) for one to treat another paternalistically. There must be a usurpation of decision making, either by preventing people from doing what they have decided or by interfering with the way in which they arrive at their decisions.

An implication of this view is that there are no methods of influencing people that are necessarily immune to being used paternalistically. It is not as if rational argument cannot be paternalistic while brute force must be. Some people may want to make their decisions impulsively, without rational deliberation; insisting that they hear arguments (for their own good) is paternalism. On the other hand, brute force used to prevent someone from crossing a washed-out bridge need not be paternalism.

What we must ascertain in each case is whether the act in question constitutes an attempt to substitute one person's judgment for another's, to promote the latter's benefit.

It is because of the violation of the autonomy of others that normative questions about the justification of paternalism arise. The denial of autonomy is inconsistent with having others share the ends of one's actions – for if they would share the end, it would not be necessary to usurp their decision-making powers. At one

123

level, therefore, paternalism seems to treat others as means (with the important difference that it is as a means to their ends, not ours). But, at the same time, because we know that the relation between the good of a person and what that person wants is not a simple one, because what is in a person's interests is not always what satisfies his or her current desires, and because we can conceive of situations in which we would want to have our autonomy denied, the possibility of justifying some paternalistic intervention will arise.

One useful heuristic to guide our judgments about the justifiability of such intervention is to ask under what conditions does A's attempts to substitute his or her judgment for B's constitute treating B as less than a moral equal.

II

It is useful to distinguish between "hard" and "soft" paternalism. Soft paternalism is the view that (1) paternalism is sometimes justified, and (2) it is a necessary condition for such justification that the person for whom we are acting paternalistically is in some way not competent. This is the view defended by Joel Feinberg in his article "Legal Paternalism."[5] More precisely, his view is slightly stronger because the necessary condition is either that the conduct in question be substantially nonvoluntary, or that we need time to determine whether the conduct is voluntary or not. Hard paternalism is the view that paternalism is sometimes justified even if the action is fully voluntary.

In arguing for a "hypothetical consent" scheme for justifying paternalism, I did not make clear whether I regarded the argument as *always* resting upon some deficiency in competence against which we wished to protect ourselves. I spoke of "irrational propensities, deficiencies in cognition and emotional capacities, and avoidable and unavoidable ignorance" as being rational reasons for agreeing (hypothetically) to limitations of our conduct, even when others' interests are not affected. I also spoke of insuring ourselves against making decisions that are "far-reaching, potentially dangerous, and irreversible." One set of considerations focuses on the agent; the

---

5 Joel Feinberg, "Legal Paternalism," *Canadian Journal of Philosophy* 1 (1977), 106–24.

other on the character of the decision. The former raises questions of rationality and competence; the latter of danger and harm.

The example of forcing people to wear seat-belts illustrates the difficulty I felt both about the correctness of paternalistic intervention and about the proper basis for its justification in such cases. Because I felt that intervention was legitimate, I sought to show that persons who do not fasten their seat-belts (at least most of them) are in some way failing in rationality. They either put an unreasonably high negative weight on what is at most an inconvenience, or discount unreasonably the probability or seriousness of future injury.

I think now that the issue must be faced more squarely. Although it is possible to relate such cases to the soft paternalistic thesis by claiming ignorance or weakness of the will, the strategy seems too ad hoc to be convincing. In any case, there will be other situations (for example, not allowing individuals to become slaves) in which this approach seems implausible. I propose, therefore, to consider three cases that are difficult for the soft paternalist, and to examine the strategies for dealing with them.

The first set of cases I shall call "safety cases." These include requiring motorcyclists to wear helmets, hunters to wear brightly colored jackets, sailors to carry life-preservers, and drivers to wear seat-belts. These are all instances of making people buy and use various items. They also include cases of preventing people from buying and using various things – bans on Red Dye No. 2, firecrackers, heroin.

The second set of cases is illustrated by the issue of putting fluoride in the community water supply. These cases differ from safety cases because, for example, we do not *require* anybody to drink fluoridated water. We just make it easy for those who wish to receive fluoride to do so and we make it correspondingly more difficult for those who do not wish to do so to avoid it. Because the argument for such measures involves a claim that there are certain actions that should be done collectively, I shall refer to these cases as "collective decisions."

The third set of cases are those forbidding people to sell themselves into slavery or to sell body parts to others. I shall refer to such cases as "slavery cases."

For all three types of cases I shall be making the assumption that there is no convincing reason for regarding the actions of the parties (not to wear helmets, not to be fluoridated, to enter into slavery) as necessarily less than voluntary.

Therefore, if one believes that the restrictive actions are justified, and if one believes that the justification is at least in part paternalistic, we have test cases for soft paternalism.

Of course, one can reject these as counterexamples by claiming that it would be wrong or unjustifiable to prevent people from becoming slaves or to force sailors to carry life-preservers. I confess that I do not see how to progress further with the argument if this is the point of disagreement. These judgments (that it is wrong to prevent people from becoming slaves, etc.) are part of a perfectly consistent position and one that is not in any way crazy. Of course, those who accept this consequence may do so because they are convinced on independent grounds that hard paternalism is unjustifiable. If so, one may be able to show that their arguments are not sound. But if the disagreement centers on these intuitions, I find it hard to see how it can be resolved.

The first strategy is to argue that the assumption I make about the cases is not valid. Anybody who would agree to become a slave or who would object to carrying a life-preserver must be in some way distracted, misinformed, impetuous, weak-willed, self-destructive, or so forth. In effect, this move denies that these are test-cases for soft paternalism. The contention seems implausible. One cannot argue a priori that persons who do such things are acting nonvoluntarily. Nothing in the concept of becoming a slave prohibits one doing this freely.

Although there might be empirical evidence for the nonvoluntary character of many such actions, it is unlikely that all such acts will be nonvoluntary. I do not see how one can rule out the possibility that hard paternalism may be the only position that can justify restrictions on such actions.

The most likely response is that while interference may be justified in such cases, it may be for nonpaternalistic reasons. The justification is based on the interests of third parties who are affected in ways that they have a right to be protected against.

The argument in the "safety" cases is that persons who are injured or killed because of their risky behavior impose costs on the rest of us. When the costs are economic, such as the costs of medical care, the obvious reply is that this might show that we can require

126

such individuals to purchase medical insurance, but it does not show that we can require them actually to wear safety helmets.

Note that in purely economic terms it is quite likely that the effect of requiring motorcycle helmets is to cause badly injured persons to survive (requiring costly medical care) who otherwise might have died from head injuries!

If the costs result from the efforts involved in rescue operations and so forth, one could again require compensation for such efforts as a matter of contract or tort law. But there will be certain individuals who intentionally or otherwise will not insure themselves and who may not be in a position to make financial compensation.

What do we do in the case of such individuals? The libertarian answer is that we announce ahead of time that such individuals will not be aided by us. But surely this imposes a psychic cost on us – that of ignoring or abandoning people in distress. There does seem to be an argument for interference here, because the rest of us do not want to be put in such a position.

In the case of hunters who are shot by other hunters because they do not wear brightly colored clothing, there is another kind of cost. People have to bear the knowledge that they have caused harm (perhaps death) to another.

Ultimately I am left with the feeling that these arguments either are not relevant to justifying restrictions on behavior (although they may justify compulsory insurance) or, if they are relevant, do not seem strong enough to tip the scale by themselves. In the final analysis, I think we are justified in requiring sailors to take along life-preservers because it minimizes the risk of harm to them at the cost of a trivial interference with their freedom.

The second set of cases, those of "collective decisions," create difficulties for any consent scheme that requires unanimous consent; it is implausible to suppose that one can argue for the rationality of such consent without making various ad hoc assumptions about the extent to which we share common values, religious outlooks, and risk-taking preferences.

We are faced with the following problem. Suppose that most people in a community would consent to a certain practice, but a minority would not. Although the best solution would be to exempt the minority, considerations of administrative and economic efficiency may make this solution very expensive. It is both more effective and cheaper to put fluoride in the community water supply than it is to distribute fluoride pills to those who want them or to supply nonfluoridated water to those who do not want fluoride.

If justice takes precedence over efficiency, the solution is clear. But this is not a question of determining the basic structure of society. It is more a constitutional question of deciding what powers to give the legislature. I am inclined to think that some balancing of interests is appropriate here. Knowing that we will be in the minority on some issues, and the majority on others, it is reasonable not to demand unanimity for certain issues.

The relevant conditions are: (1) that the majority interest must be important (such as health); (2) that the imposition on the minority must be relatively minor (they have to buy their own water); and (3) that the administrative and economic costs of not imposing on the minority would be very high. However, fairness requires that if there are economic costs to the minority (such as purchasing nonfluoridated water), they should be borne by those who gain.

In this analysis, the restriction on the minority is not motivated by paternalistic considerations, but by the interests of a majority who wish to promote their own welfare. Hence, these are not paternalistic decisions, and do not count against soft paternalism.

Finally, we come to "slavery cases," in which people are not allowed to enter into certain voluntary agreements that would result in great loss of liberty or serious risk of bodily injury. While there may be a presumption in light of what we know about human nature that such choices are usually not fully voluntary, this is a presumption that may be rebutted in particular cases. These are also difficult cases for soft paternalism.

In these cases, however, there is a different line of argument open to the soft paternalist. Because the issue is whether a certain contract will be enforced rather than whether there will be a first-order restriction on the conduct itself, one might argue that different principles apply. Refusal to enforce such agreements may frustrate desires, but it is not a direct interference with liberty.

Again, one may look for third-party considerations. Most of us do not want to live in a society in which, for example, we are legally obligated to return runaway slaves to their owners. Such considerations underlie the general doctrine in contract law that does not require specific performance for the breach of a personal-service contract..

128

In my original paper, I argued that our objection to allowing voluntary slavery was linked to the promotion of the very value against which paternalism offends – autonomy. If we conceive of autonomy as the capacity of individuals to critically reflect on and take responsibility for the kind of persons they want to be, then we stop people from becoming slaves in order to preserve their future ability to define the kind of lives they want to lead. Although I still find this argument plausible, my more recent reflections on autonomy raise the following theoretical problem. There is nothing in the idea of autonomy that precludes a person from saying, "I want to be the kind of person who acts at the command of others. I define myself as a slave and endorse those attitudes and preferences. My autonomy consists in being a slave."

If this is coherent, and I think it is, one cannot argue against such slavery on grounds of autonomy. The argument will have to appeal to some idea of what is a fitting life for a person and, thus, be a direct attempt to impose a conception of what is "good" on another person.

If, as I suspect, any person who adopted the above attitude would argue for it on grounds of maximizing some other good, the case may reduce to a safety-case as one of mistaken calculation about the best way of securing a person's good as conceived by her or him. The hard theoretical position may never be reached.[6]

6 I would like to thank Daniel Brock, Leslie Francis, and Eric Mack for helpful comments on an earlier draft.

9

The serpent beguiled me and I did eat: entrapment and the creation of crime

In the past few years a number of criminal prosecutions have brought to public attention the issue of entrapment: Abscam, the DeLorean cocaine trial, Operation Greylord, various sting fencing operations. The investigative techniques used in, say, Abscam, although highly elaborate, expensive, and ingenious are only one example of the range of investigative techniques with which I shall be concerned in this essay. What these techniques have in common is the use of deception to produce the performance of a criminal act under circumstances in which it can be observed by law enforcement officials. I shall use the term "pro-active enforcement" to cover such techniques and the question I shall be discussing is under what circumstances, if any, is the use of such measures legitimate.

I

Let me begin by saying something more about the nature of pro-active law enforcement and also by giving a fairly extensive sample of the use of such techniques. The sample will not only make clearer the nature of such operations but also provide a range of cases for testing judgments about the acceptability of such techniques.

Traditionally, law enforcement in our society has left most of the burden of reporting criminal offenses to private citizens. It is left to individuals, usually victims, to come forward with a complaint of criminal action and to provide much of the evidence in identifying and prosecuting the criminal. Government's role has been limited to various patrol activities and to reaction to complaint. Hence, the traditional notion of reactive law enforcement.

This chapter was originally published in *Law and Philosophy* 4 (May 1985), 17–39, © 1985 by D. Reidel Publishing Company. Reprinted by permission.

Recently the existence of "invisible offenses" has posed challenges to reactive law enforcement. Invisible offenses include not only the so-called victimless crimes, that is, those crimes in which there are no complaints because all parties to the transaction are willing (drugs, vice, gambling) but also a variety of cases in which the victims are not aware of any criminal act. The patrons of a hotel are not aware of code violations whose existence is protected by the bribery of a building inspector. The purchasers of General Electric products were not aware of the fact that the price of the products they bought was affected by a price-fixing agreement. The customers of a bank are not aware of the loss of funds due to the embezzlement of a teller. There is another class of offenses that produces knowing victims but where, for a variety of reasons, the victims are not prepared to complain – blackmail, extortion, sexual harassment. We know from crime surveys that many victims of robbery and theft do not report these crimes either because of fear of harassment or because they believe it to be a waste of time.

Faced with the failure of the traditional modes of notification and investigative aid, law enforcement officials have turned to modes of investigation in which the reporting, observation, and testimony can be done by the officials themselves. Detection of crime and investigation of crime proceed simultaneously. This is the arena of pro-active law enforcement. Originally used mainly in drug and vice investigations, such techniques are now being used increasingly for many other kinds of crime. I shall enumerate a list of such techniques.

Decoy operations. The New York City Street Crime Unit is a unit of the New York City Police Department that specializes in the techniques of "decoying and blending." The decoy is a police officer who assumes the role of a potential victim. He (or she) may play the role of derelict, shopper, grandmother, drunk, "john," cab driver, potential rape victim. The decoy is placed in an area where experience indicates it is likely the decoy will become a victim. The back-up blends into the street area near the decoy. When the decoy indicates that a crime has been committed the back-up team moves in for the arrest. A similar idea using inanimate objects occurs when decoy letters are sent to trap postal thieves.

In most decoy cases the potential offender is not targeted. But the same techniques can be used against specific suspects. In one case a Manhattan dentist was targeted after three patients had complained that they had been molested while under anaesthesia. An undercover policewoman posed as a patient, accepted anaesthesia, and was kept under surveillance by a hidden camera. The dentist was arrested and the video evidence led to a conviction.

Sting operations. Undercover agents take over a warehouse and announce that they are in the market to purchase stolen goods. They purchase goods brought to them and, after some period of time, arrest the sellers of the stolen property. Similar operations have involved running a pornographic bookstore in order to arrest film wholesalers.

Manna from heaven operations. Police leave a piece of luggage unattended at the Port Authority bus terminal and arrest those who attempt to walk off with it. As an integrity test for policemen money is left in an apartment, the door is left open, and an "open-door" call is put through to the police.

Honey-pot operations. Undercover agents provide opportunities for various criminal acts without actively soliciting them. They may, for example, open a garbage business in the hopes of becoming targets for extortion, or operate a bar in the hopes of being solicited for bribes by city inspectors.

Solicitation operations. The most common mode of drug enforcement involves government agents offering to buy drugs from dealers. Similar methods are used to enforce laws against counterfeit currency and illegal firearms. In one of the more creative uses of such techniques, the police fencing detail in Portland, Oregon purchased color television sets at wholesale prices (under an LEAA grant) and then made the rounds of bars offering to sell the sets very cheaply, claiming they were stolen. As part of the same operation, randomly chosen appliance stores were approached with the same offer.

In the recent Operation Greylord in Cook County, Illinois, undercover agents staged a crime and arrest so that they could solicit offers to drop the charges for a payment.

In the course of soliciting a crime the government may play an active role in a criminal operation. In one extreme case involving liquor regulations, an agent contacted two defendants with whom

132

he had been previously involved in the production of bootleg alcohol and pressured them to reestablish operations. He offered to provide a still, a still-site, equipment, and an operator. He then provided two thousand pounds of sugar at wholesale. The operation lasted for three years during which the government agent was the only customer.

Although the Ninth Circuit reversed this conviction, it did not do so on grounds of entrapment. It did argue, however, that "the same underlying objections which render entrapment objectionable to American criminal justice are operative."[1] To see both why the court did not find entrapment, and what the underlying objectives referred to consist in, we must now examine the nature of the entrapment defense. Although my concern is with the normative issues raised by pro-active law enforcement, the legal doctrine of entrapment has been the focus of much of the discussion of such issues, and many of the conceptual and normative distinctions are present in the legal discussion.

II

Entrapment is a defense to a criminal charge. The defendant asserts a claim that he ought not to be held legally liable for some criminal act. It is a defense that originally was a judicial creation although it has since been codified in a number of states including Illinois, New York, and Alaska. It is also interesting to note that as a bar to criminal liberty it is virtually exclusive to the criminal jurisprudence of the United States.

It is a very narrow defense in that it only applies when the entrapment is performed by a government agent. It is not available to those who are enticed into criminal acts by private citizens. The term "government agents," however, includes all employees of government, and in certain circumstances private citizens working for a government agent will count as government agents.

Entrapment occurs when government agents procure the commission of a criminal act by someone who, except for the solicitation, persuasion, or enticement, would not have committed the crime. Both the conditions under which entrapment will be found and the theoretical foundations of the defense are matters of legal

1 Green v. United States, 454 F. 2nd 783 (9th Cir. 1971).

dispute. Originally, state and federal courts based the defense on estoppel and public policy. But in 1932 the Supreme Court replaced these with the legal fiction that Congress implicitly excludes entrapment whenever it enacts a criminal statute. The court held that if the police implant in the mind of an innocent person the disposition to commit an offense it is unfair to find such a person guilty. We see here two elements that recur through the future development of the doctrine – the innocence or predisposition of the offender and the inducement to commit the offense.

Sorrels v. United States contains the two main views about the justification of the entrapment defense.[2] The majority focuses on entrapment as a defense in the standard sense of the term, that is, as a factor affecting the culpability or innocence of the offender. If somebody is found innocent by virtue of entrapment then, on this view, it is similar to being found innocent by virtue of mistake of fact. The offender is not, or not as, culpable. As an excuse, entrapment is focused on the conduct of the defendant and his relative blameworthiness.

The concurring view, on the other hand, focuses not on the culpability of the offender but on the integrity of the judicial process and the legitimacy of the methods used by the police. The defendant is excused, not because he is less culpable, but because the government has acted in an illegitimate fashion. The point of the defense is not to exculpate offenders but to monitor police behavior.

Parallel to these different views of the nature and function of the defense has been the development of two different standards for the applicability of the defense. What has come to be called the "subjective" test concentrates on the offender's state of mind. With whom did the intent to commit the crime originate? Was the defendant predisposed to commit the crime? Would this particular defendant have committed this particular crime in the absence of the government's conduct? On the view that the defense affects culpability, only those not predisposed to commit the offense will be excused. That is why the defendant in Greene, who had a prior history of violation of liquor regulations, could not invoke entrapment.

The "objective" test, sometimes called the "hypothetical person" test, focuses on the conduct of the police, not the defendant. It asks

2 Sorrells v. United States, 287 U.S. 435 (1932).

whether the methods used would have led a hypothetical law-abiding citizen to commit the crime in question. As the California Supreme Court put it:

[We] are not concerned with who first conceived or who willingly, reluctantly, acquiesced in a criminal project. What we do care about is how much and what manner of persuasion, pressure and cajoling are brought to bear by law enforcement officials to induce persons to commit crime . . . The proper test of entrapment in California is the following: was the conduct of the law-enforcement agent likely to induce a normally law-abiding person to commit the offense.[3]

Note that on this view it does not matter whether or not this defendant was predisposed. If a hypothetical nonpredisposed person would have been likely to commit the crime because of the actions of the police, this defendant is let off, not because he is innocent, but because the government conduct cannot be condoned.

The two views cannot be integrated into a single theory. For on the view that emphasizes the innocence of those induced to perform criminal acts it should be irrelevant whether or not the entrapping parties are government agents or private citizens. And on the view that emphasizes the conduct of government agents, it should be irrelevant whether or not the suspect was predisposed to commit the crime.

Because the dominant opinion in the Supreme Court has favored the subjective test of entrapment, and most defendants have a criminal record, which makes it difficult to demonstrate lack of predisposition, the entrapment defense remains limited in scope, rarely used, and even less rarely successful.

The legal literature on entrapment consists almost exclusively in exposition of the Supreme Court's various views about the doctrine, and normative questions are usually confined to arguing the relative merits of subjective versus objective tests.[4] The much larger and important issue of the legitimacy of government-created crime is ignored. What values are threatened by the use of pro-active methods of law enforcement? Ought we to distinguish between public officials and private citizens as targets of such techniques?

3 People v. Barraza, 23 Cal. 3rd 675 (1979).
4 Some exceptions include Park, *The Entrapment Controversy*, 60 Minn. L. Rev. 163 (1976); Goldstein, *For Harold Laswell: Some Reflections on Human Dignity. Entrapment, Informed Consent and the Plea Bargain*, 84 Yale L.J. 683 (1975); *Causation and Intention in the Entrapment Defense*, 28 UCLA Law J. 859 (1981).

Ought criminals have a right to complain about efficient methods of investigating and detecting their crimes? If certain crimes, for example, bribery, can only (or most efficiently) be detected by these methods then does a norm of equal enforcement of the law favor such techniques?

III

The central moral concern with pro-active law enforcement techniques is that they manufacture or create crime in order that offenders be prosecuted and punished. They do not discover criminal activity; they create it. I take it that there is some common understanding of these terms such that if this were an accurate and apt description of certain law-enforcement methods there would be a decisive objection to their use.

Consider, for example, the scenario of U.S. v. Ordner.[5] Ordner, a commercial blaster and firearms manufacturer, with no previous history of lawbreaking, was approached by a government informer at a gun show. The informer, working with the government in the hope of reducing his sentence in a pending case, offered to introduce Ordner to a contractor who might have some blasting work for him. When Ordner went to meet the contractor, he was instead confronted with an elaborate scheme concocted by agents of the Bureau of Alcohol, Tax and Firearms to resemble a meeting of an underworld gang. Ordner eventually provided the blueprint and directed the assembly of five hundred "penguns." This is clearly an instance of the creation of criminal activity by law-enforcement agents. What are the elements that distinguish the creation or manufacture of crime from its investigation and detection?

If one looks back at the range of operations listed earlier, one sees that there are various means by which agents contrive to have criminal acts performed in their presence (other than maintaining surveillance of the suspect or a potential crime scene). They can suggest the crime be committed, offer various incentives, use coercion, provide some of the means needed to commit the crime, participate in the commission of the crime, arrange the presence of a potential victim, arrange the presence of a valuable object in an

5 554 F. 2d 24 (2d. Circ.), 434 U.S. 824 (1977).

unsecure context, offer to buy or sell contraband, appeal to sentiments of friendship.

On at least one view all of these might count as the creation of criminal activity. Suppose we defined the creation of criminal activity as occurring whenever the police acted in such a way that they caused criminal activity to occur. According to one idea of cause that has played an important role in tort law, one event is said to cause another if it is a necessary condition for its occurrence. This is referred to as "but for" causation. But for the presence of the event in question the other event would not have occurred. Now it is a feature of all pro-active techniques that but for the actions of law enforcement officials the crime for which the defendants are charged would, almost certainly, not have been committed.

Thus, if a policeman rides on a bus with a wallet in his back pocket, and his pocket is picked, but for the actions of the policeman his wallet would not have been stolen. If an officer, suspecting short weighting, makes a purchase of meat at a supermarket, weighs it, and finds it short weighted, then this particular fraudulent sale would not have been committed if the government had not acted. Yet, in these cases, it does not seem that the culpability of defendants is reduced, or that the methods go beyond some idea of what is fair.

One way to see this is to note that in an ordinary mugging the presence of the victim is a but for cause of the crime. If this little old lady had not been walking her dog in the park, her mugging would not have occurred. But, surely, she did not create or manufacture crime. The contribution of the state has to go beyond simply providing a potential victim, as in decoy operations.

If, however, the decoy is made to look particularly vulnerable and the "reward" particularly attractive, then questions of temptation and the overcoming of the will raise issues of causation and responsibility. If the crime is made sufficiently "easier" or sufficiently attractive then, as social scientists who leave wallets lying about in phone booths find out, almost any of us is likely to commit a crime.

It is relevant here to note that the increased probability does not occur simply as a foreseen consequence of governmental action. A case of this would be the decision to shift patrols to a high-crime area foreseeing that there would be an increase in crime in the section

137

of town with reduced patrols. But, in the case we are considering, the point of the action is to increase the likelihood that a crime will be committed in the presence of the police.

If somebody commits a crime, and would not have done so absent the efforts of the state to make the crime easier, has the state created crime? To help in thinking about this let us look at other parts of the law that have developed theory on similar matters. In tort law it is common to invoke the idea that if one neglects to take precautions against harm one is liable for the harm that comes about, even if the harm is brought about by others. Thus a house painter was held liable for the loss of goods stolen by a thief who entered when the painter failed to lock the front door. But the language of the courts in such cases is not that the negligent party causes the wrongdoer to do what he does, or that he causes the harm that results. Rather it is that one has a duty to guard against such harm. Providing others with the opportunity to do harm may ground liability but not because it causes the harm.

In the criminal law there is also a distinction drawn between providing an opportunity to commit a crime and inducing others to commit crime. With respect to criminal responsibility, a person is only held to have caused another to act if he makes use of threats, lies, or the exercise of authority to induce another to act.

With respect to civil liability for the acts of others, the accepted view is that one individual must do something that is directly addressed to the other person such as uttering a threat, or making a false statement, or exploiting personal influence. It is only when the agent led to act is less than fully competent, as in the case of young children, that the mere providing of a temptation counts as causing another to act – as in the doctrine of "attractive nuisance."

Both on grounds of conformity with other legal doctrine and harmony with common sense notions of causation, it is reasonable not to count the mere provision of opportunity to commit a crime as the manufacture or creation of crime. It is only if the opportunity is made sufficiently attractive that creation of opportunities can be regarded as temptation. The danger of such techniques is that they may lead persons to commit crimes who have not engaged in similar activities before. The person who walks away with the "abandoned" suitcase in the Port Authority building may not have been disposed to steal anything at all. In such cases there is the danger

138

that one may not merely shift the scene of criminal activity but create crime that otherwise would not have occurred.

The offer to buy drugs, sex, or stolen goods from those already engaged in their sale, or letting it be known that one is available for a bribe, does more than merely make it easier to commit a crime. It invites the criminal to act. Again, this does not seem sufficient to categorize the activity as the creation of crime because, although the particular sale might not have taken place had it not been for the offer to engage in the transaction, by hypothesis one is dealing with those already engaged in criminal activity. Leaving aside complications, such as the fact that sting fencing operations may encourage individuals to commit burglaries by providing a ready outlet at above-market prices, such offers are on the portion of the spectrum closer to shifting the scene of criminal activity.

An interesting comparison is between the offer to sell as opposed to buy contraband. This seems a more questionable practice but it is not apparent where the difference lies. It is a crime to buy as well as sell contraband. Both transactions rely on the willingness of an offender to engage in the transaction. Although it is true that the danger to society is usually greater from the seller than the buyer, this seems to be relevant to what crimes to aim at, not at which techniques are permissible. Moreover, it does not seem particularly outrageous to let it be known that one is willing to sell one's services as a contract murderer (for the purpose of apprehending a buyer of such services).

I believe this is explained by the contingent fact that the offer to sell is more likely to be made without knowledge that a particular individual is already embarked on a course of criminal conduct. This is why the Oregon case of going into bars and offering to sell supposedly stolen televisions seems to be the creation of crime, whereas the offer to sell one's services as a contract murderer does not. In the former the state is, in effect, making a random test of the corruptibility of the general public.

The next step up from merely providing an opportunity, or merely offering to engage in a criminal transaction, is to provide the necessary means for the commission of a crime. Consider for example the facts in the Twigg case.[6] Robert Kubica, after being

6 U.S. v. Twigg, 558 F. 2d 373 (3d Cir. 1978).

arrested on charges of illegally manufacturing speed, pled guilty and agreed to assist the Drug Enforcement Administration in prosecuting other offenders. At the request of DEA officials, he contacted an acquaintance, Henry Neville, and proposed that they set up a laboratory for manufacturing speed. Kubica assumed responsibility for acquiring the necessary equipment, raw materials, and a production site. The DEA supplied all of these plus an ingredient essential to the manufacture that, while legal, was difficult to obtain. Twigg joined the operation at the invitation of Neville. Kubica alone had the technical knowledge and skills necessary to manufacture the drug and had complete charge of the laboratory. The Court reversed on the grounds that when Kubica contacted him, Neville

was not engaged in any illicit drug activity. Using Kubica, and actively participating with him, the DEA agents deceptively implanted the criminal design in Neville's mind... This egregious conduct on the part of government agents generated new crimes by the defendant merely for the sake of pressing criminal charges against him when, as far as the record reveals, he was lawfully and peacefully minding his own affairs. Fundamental fairness does not permit us to countenance such actions by law enforcement officials and prosecution for a crime so fomented will be barred.[7]

I should suppose fundamental fairness would raise some problems about this case even if the intent to commit the crime arose in Neville. Imagine that he approached Kubica saying he would like to manufacture some speed but, unfortunately, lacked the raw materials, the technical skills, the capital, and the equipment. Kubica then supplies them all and Neville is then arrested. What is the harm that the state seeks to avoid by such prosecutions?

Nevertheless the court is focusing on the right factor in the creation of crime – the origin of criminal intent. The essential question for determining when crime has been created is what the role of government is in causing the offender to form the specific intent to commit the crime in question. The issue of predisposition, which runs through the entrapment commentary, is a red herring. We are not interested in the general willingness of an offender to commit crime but in whether he has formed the intent to engage in a specific crime if the opportunity presents itself. In so far as only an opportunity is offered, then if the offender is using it to realize a

7 U.S. v. Twigg, at 381.

preexisting purpose, the origin of intent is in him. If the government, in Learned Hand's phrase, "solicits, proposes, initiates, broaches or suggests" the offense then the origin of the intent lodges with the state.

Real situations are, of course, complicated by overdetermination. Suppose, for example, I form the intent to commit a crime if and only if I am solicited to do so by someone else. Or suppose I form the intent to steal something, but cannot overcome a residual fear of being apprehended, and it is only your encouragement that enables me to carry out the original intent.

The fact that there are difficult questions about determining the origin of intent only shows that the question of whether crime has been manufactured is often hard to settle. And that is something we already knew. If the ambiguities and difficulties in determining the origin of intent match those in deciding whether crime has been created, that is all one can demand in terms of a satisfactory analysis.

Given our understanding of the idea of the creation of crime in terms of origin of intent, we can now pass to the normative issues. Is it legitimate, and if so under what conditions, for the government to create criminal activity?

IV

To answer this question one must have some general view about the underlying purpose and rules of fairness that are embedded in the particular system of criminal law enforcement we have adopted. The legitimacy of particular law-enforcement techniques is necessarily relative to a particular conception or model of criminal justice. At most an argument for condemning particular modes of enforcement will be of the form "If you accept a particular ideal of the purposes and fairness of attaching criminal sanctions to rules of conduct, then these methods will be inconsistent or not cohere with such an ideal."

I shall sketch the outlines of what I believe to be an ideal of the principles of distribution applied to criminal sanctions embedded in our current practice and jurisprudence.

1. Criminal sanctions constitute an interference with the liberty of the members of a society.

2. They are justified, at least in part, by their contribution to the adherence of citizens to justifiable standards of conduct.
3. Individuals ought to have a broad area of autonomy, that is, self-determination, in the choice of behavior and the formation of goals and purposes.
4. There is a conflict between maximizing autonomy and promoting fundamental human goods such as security of possessions, personal integrity, and opportunity. One way of mitigating this conflict is to allow individuals to choose whether or not to become subject to criminal sanctions by presenting them with reasons against certain conduct (sanctions) and letting them make the decisions to comply or not. Individuals who are legitimately punished have self-selected themselves for such treatment.
5. The criminal law is not to be thought of as a price system, that is, as it being indifferent whether a citizen obeys the law or violates it but pays the price of the sanction. The criminal law is meant to be obeyed. Certain behaviors are forbidden and others are required, and although the citizen is given a choice (in the sense that the behaviors are not made impossible), his will is constrained to make the correct choice.

These propositions have implications for very different aspects of the criminal-justice system. They affect the substantive content of legal standards; for example, standards that are very difficult or impossible to obey would be ruled out. They affect procedural issues, for example, laws should be prospective in application. They affect the excusing conditions we ought to allow. And they affect the types of law-enforcement techniques we should regard as legitimate.

In light of the above propositions the normative issue may be phrased in the following manner: What methods of apprehending and detecting offenders are consistent with the view of a system of criminal sanctions as a choosing system and as the enforcement of law, that is, authoritative rules backed by sanctions. I am claiming that it is not consistent with such a system that law-enforcement officials attempt to see if they can cause a person to commit a crime by suggesting or encouraging in any way that a crime be committed.

It is not that such suggestions are improper only if they are such as to overwhelm the will. The use of coercion, excessive temptation, and fraud are obviously inconsistent with the view that we are only entitled to punish those offenders who willingly choose to commit crimes. I am arguing for the much stronger view that it is not proper to solicit, encourage, or suggest crime even if this is done by no stronger means than verbal suggestion. It is not that the offender can complain after the fact that his will was overborne. It is that we, any of us, can complain before the fact that it is not the purpose of officers of the law to encourage crime for the purpose of punishing it.

For the law is set up to forbid people to engage in certain kinds of behavior. In effect it is commanding "Do not do this." And it shows that it is commanding, as opposed to requesting or advising by saying that it will impose sanctions on those who refuse to conform. It will "humble the will," to use H. Fingarette's language.[8]

But for a law-enforcement official to encourage, suggest, or invite crime is to, in effect, be saying "Do this." It is certainly unfair to the citizen to be invited to do that which the law forbids him to do. But it is more than unfair; it is conceptually incoherent. Of course this incoherence does not appear to the person being entrapped because he is not aware of the official capacity of his entrapper. And the incapacity is concealed from the official because he thinks of himself as trying to detect a criminal – the thought being that an honest citizen will simply refuse the invitation. From the standpoint of one trying to understand and evaluate the system, however, the conflict is clear.

It is important to note that we are not literally involved in a contradiction as we would be, for example, if the Statutes both commanded and forbade that a certain action be done. Nor is it a pragmatic contradiction, in the sense of being self-defeating. The person who says "P but I do not believe P" takes back with the latter part of his assertion what he implies with the former part. Nor is it self-defeating in the sense that it cannot be useful to engage in such behavior in order to increase overall compliance with the legal system. It is not as if one part of the criminal justice system (the police) are trying to undo what another part (the legislature) is trying to accomplish.

It is not always incoherent to invite someone to do the very act that one is trying to get them to avoid doing. Consider a parent trying to teach a child not to touch the stove. In the case of a particularly recalcitrant child the most effective technique might be

8 H. Fingarette, "Punishment and Suffering," *Proceedings and Addresses of the American Philosophical Society* 50 (1977), 510.

to encourage the child to touch the stove in one's presence. The slight pain now will teach the child to avoid a greater pain later. But this is surely not the model being used by the police. They are interested either in deterring others or in punishing guilty people. The end being served is not that of the person being invited to commit the crime.

I suppose we can (barely) make sense of a system of rules forbidding certain behavior that is enforced by inviting people to commit the forbidden acts and then punishing them for doing so. But such a system violates elementary standards of coherence and fairness.

To encourage the commission of a crime in the absence of any reason to believe the individual is already engaged in a course of criminal conduct is to be a tester of virtue, not a detector of crime.

As a way of insuring against such testing of virtue, I suggest that whenever the action of creating an intent to commit a criminal act would render a private citizen liable to criminal charges as accessory or coconspirator, public officials should be allowed to perform such acts as would create such an intent only if they have probable cause to suppose that the individuals approached are already engaged or are intending to engage in activity of a similar nature. If they offer to buy contraband from specific individuals, they should have probable cause to believe those individuals are already engaged in such transactions. If they offer to sell stolen goods to individuals, they ought to have probable cause to believe such individuals are already buying stolen goods. If they offer bribes to public officials, then they should have probable cause to suppose that the officials are already corrupt; not just corruptible.

To use an analogy, we do not think it proper for police to engage in random searches of homes in order to detect possible criminal activity. Why then should we allow random solicitation or encouragement of criminal activity? I have heard it argued that, on grounds of equitable law enforcement, it is wrong to allow those who may have corrupt dispositions, but have been fortunate enough not to have been given the opportunity to exercise them, to escape punishment when their less fortunate counterparts are caught. After all if we had offered them a bribe they would have taken it. This counter-factual seems to me an interesting piece of data for God, but not for the FBI. Suggesting the commission of a crime, even

144

to wicked people, is not a legitimate function of a system of law enforcement.[9,10]

Although my discussion has been much broader than the topic of Abscam, I would like to apply the discussion to Abscam, partly because it has caused so much controversy and partly because it is a difficult case to form a judgment about. Abscam is not one case but many because there were a number of different public officials involved. But basically the actual solicitation of crime involved either offering money to secure residency for the "sheik" or the offer to finance a titanium mine in return for using political office to secure government contracts. It is the latter case (Senator Williams) that I wish to focus upon.

The charges against Williams and his attorney related to a titanium mine and processing plant. Williams's investment group, consisting of himself, his attorney Feinberg, Katz, Errichetti (the mayor of Camden), and Sandy Williams, sought financing to acquire the titanium enterprise. Through Errichetti the group contacted Melvin Weinberg, a convicted swindler who was working for the government, and an undercover agent, Anthony Amoroso. The latter pair posed as members of Abdul Enterprises, an investment firm pre-

9 I have ignored in my argument any discussion of the practical consequences of law-enforcement officials engaging in the creation of crime. My argument has been addressed to matters of principle rather than practice. I believe, however, that considerations of likely consequences strengthens the argument. The work of Gary Marx, a sociologist from MIT, is the best source for the dangers of undercover police work in general. Here are some of the problems that he worries about: (a) the lack of effective supervision of informers and police; (b) the possibility of damage to unwitting victims and third parties; (c) the possibility of police participating in real crimes to gain the confidence of the targeted suspects; (d) the use of selective targeting against political opponents; (e) the corrupting effect on police of pretending to be corrupt; (f) excessive invasion of privacy; (g) stimulation of criminal activity, for example, through offering to purchase stolen goods.

10 A version of this paper was read at the Eastern Division Meetings of the American Philosophical Association. My commentators at the meeting were Gerald Postema and Patricia White. I am indebted to them, and in particular to Postema, for helpful suggestions and criticisms. I wish to express my gratitude to the Hastings Center where this essay began while I was in residence as a Luce Senior Scholar.

tending to represent wealthy Arabs. Criminal charges arose out of the promise requested by the undercover agent as a condition for the financing, that Williams would use his power and influence to obtain government contracts for purchasing the titanium to be produced.

My own reading of the trial transcripts and the due process hearings that followed the conviction of Williams convinces me that Senator Williams acted in a corrupt and morally indefensible manner. Quite independently of the outcome of the criminal charges, the Senate Ethics Committee acted entirely correctly in recommending that Williams be expelled from the Senate – an outcome he avoided by resigning.

On the legal issue of entrapment the trial judge denied Williams's motions to dismiss the indictment on grounds of entrapment and the Supreme Court concurred. What this shows, in my view, is that the current legal doctrine of entrapment is too narrowly construed because I believe the best reading of the evidence shows that Williams' crime was created and manufactured by the state, that there was no probable cause for targeting Williams, and that, in accordance with my earlier argument, it was improper to proceed with prosecution. I can, in this appendix, only briefly highlight what I believe to be the grounds supporting my reading of the evidence. I shall be ignoring various aspects of the investigation that raise due process questions of their own, such as the reliability of Weinberg, the chief government informant, the absence of control over Weinberg by government agents, the absence of written reports summarizing conversations that were not recorded. I will focus only on the entrapment issues.

Was there probable cause for targeting Williams? The U.S. Attorney who supervised the investigation stated that he "had no reason to question the integrity of Senator Harrison Williams." The Special Agent in Charge, John Good, testified the government was "starting with a clean slate." Nowhere is there evidence of a predicate to investigate. It is the absence of such a predicate, not the question of predisposition, which I regard as crucial to the legitimacy of soliciting or encouraging crime.

As to the question of where the suggestion for criminal activity arose, one has to read the evidence and note when and how often the suggestion for illegal conduct arose with the informant or government agents. The titanium venture itself was a legitimate busi-

146

ness venture. The criminal elements included using political influence to get government contracts, concealing one's interest in the mine, and so forth. Consider these conversations. MW is Melvin Weinberg, the government informant. SW is Sandy Williams, friend and business associate of Senator Williams. TD is an FBI agent. AF is Williams's attorney and business associate, GK is a business associate of Williams.

MW: All right, now what about, uh, let me ask you a question. There's a lot of government contracts that, ya know, on the chemicals.
SW: Right.
MW: Now, can Williams get us the bids on them.
SW: Well, I don't know about that. The main thing is with this Cyanamid thing . . .
MW: Yeah.
SW: They've got customers they've had for twenty, thirty, forty years . . . And if we wanna increase our business, we'll have to, we'll have to go into like Sherman-Williams and people like that and try to get their business away from somebody else.
TD: Is he going to be able to steer any kind of contracts from the Committees that he's going to get involved with? I mean . . .
AF: Well, this I didn't know until now I have to ask him that.
GK: He's not a guy, he's not a doer, you know, quietly behind the scene, you know, he, uh, may move a little bit . . . but let me tell you this here between you and me, he's in a very, very powerful position here, the committees that he heads, you understand?
MW: Yeah.
GK: But he doesn't use that power for any advantages.
MW: Oh, how can we make him use it?

In this exchange the associates of Williams did not raise the issue of government contracts, and in every case where the government did so, they acted in a neutral or discouraging fashion. With respect to concealing his interest in the mine, notice how in this conversation between Feinberg, Weinberg, and Da Vito, the suggestion of concealing the interests arises from the government.

MW: That's in the mine though. But on the other thing there he, in fact you may we may put the 20 percent in his name even. I don't think he can though.
TD: Well, if he puts . . .
AF: I don't know, we haven't decided yet. We're gonna both examine the law involving his side investments which he . . .
MW: I don't think he can.
AF: He can put it in his wife's name or someone else.
MW: They could chase that too fast.

TD: Yeah.

MW: Come on, you're an attorney, you know that.

AF: I know that.

TD: Any, anything that he puts...

AF: I'm not sure that he's forbidden.

MW: Sure he is if he's going to get us open doors. Come on, you know that's a conflict of interest. He'll be sitting with Nixon out in Clemente there.

Perhaps the most controversial aspect of the investigation involves the coaching session between Weinberg and Williams just prior to Williams' meeting with the "sheik." This is the backstage maneuver before the on-camera performance. Here is Weinberg telling Williams what to say.

MW: Forget the mine. Don't even mention the mine... [Tell him] How high you are in the Senate... He's interested in you... Who you know in the Senate can do you favors... Without you there is no deal. You are the deal. You put this together. You worked on this and you got the government contracts. Without me there is no government contracts... Mention, you know, come on as strong as possible... You gotta just play and blow your horn. The louder you blow and mention names, who you control. And that's it, it goes no further. It's all talk, all bullshit.

But with all this effort the meeting with the sheik proves inconclusive. In November 1979, the prosecutors held a meeting to review the evidence against Williams and came to the conclusion that further investigative efforts were required.

Relative to the matter concerning US Senator Harrison Williams of New Jersey, the following was decided:

1. It will be necessary to recontact US Senator Williams to attempt to obtain an overt action on his part regarding the sponsorship of some type of legislation, i.e., tax cover for titanium mine and/or import quotas for titanium mine.

2. It was also suggested that attempts should be made to elicit from US Senator Williams whether or not he wanted his share hidden, through discussions concerning reporting of personal taxes and official acts that he promised to provide.

The prosecutors subsequently decided to add the "asylum scenario" that had been used so successfully against other Congressmen. A meeting between Williams and the sheik was held in which the sheik offered Williams money to obtain permanent residency in the United States. Williams refused the money, although he did go on to link his assistance on the immigration matter to the financing of the titanium venture. Incidentally, this meeting, which was videotaped and observed by the investigators, was interrupted at one point by a phone call by an FBI agent who instructed the sheik as to what he should say to Williams. The agent later testified as to the purpose of the interruption: "It was clear from the way the conversation was going on that it wasn't quite as specific as we would have liked it to have been."

I suggest that what we had in this case was not an investigation of whether Senator Williams was breaking the law but an effort to see if he could be induced to do so. That he was apparently quite willing to be so induced is not at issue. The issue is whether it is legitimate to substitute for the question "Is this individual, who we have reason to suspect of corrupt activity, acting in a corrupt manner?" the question "Can we corrupt this individual who we have no reason to believe is corrupt?"

I do not deny that political corruption is a very difficult crime to detect by normal investigative techniques. I also do not believe that it is impermissible to use deception and trickery in the attempt to uncover such corruption. But I do not believe that it is legitimate to solicit and encourage such corruption unless we have evidence that the targeted individuals are already engaged in such corruption.

10

Behavior control and design

What is wrong with it [the world of *Walden Two*]? Only one thing: somebody "planned it that way." If these critics had come upon a society in some remote corner of the world which boasted similar advantages, they would undoubtedly have hailed it as providing a pattern we all might well follow – provided that it was clearly the result of a natural process of cultural evolution. Any evidence that intelligence had been used in arriving at this version of the good life would, in their eyes, be a serious flaw.[1]

A cultural practice is not the less effective in determining the behavior characteristics of a group because its origins are accidental. But once the effect upon behavior has been observed, the source of the practice may be scrutinized more closely. Certain questions come to be asked. Why should the design of a culture be left so largely to accident? Is it not possible to change the social environment deliberately so that the human product will meet more acceptable specifications?[2]

In this essay I shall consider an argument that is often made in discussions of methods of influencing people's behavior. This argument states that control of one person by another is constantly taking place, but in an implicit and unconscious fashion, and that it would be preferable for control to take place on a systematic and explicit basis. Here is a small sample of these arguments.

All men control and are controlled. The question of government in the broadest possible sense is not how freedom is to be preserved but what kinds of control are to be used and to what ends.[3]

This chapter was originally published in *Social Research*, 52 (Autumn 1985), 543–54. Reprinted by permission.
1 B. F. Skinner, "Some Issues Concerning the Control of Human Behavior: A Symposium with Carl Rogers," *Science* 124 (Nov. 30, 1956), 1059.
2 B. F. Skinner, *Science and Human Behavior* (New York: Free Press, 1953), 426–7.
3 Skinner, "Some Issues," 1060.

The behavioral scientist does not confine himself to schedules of reinforcement which happen to occur in nature. . . . There is no virtue in the accidental nature of an accident . . . The intentional design of a culture and the control of human behavior it implies are essential if the human species is to continue to develop.[4]

The argument may be set out in explicit fashion as follows: (1) There is no choice to be made between modes of influence that control and those that do not. All methods of influencing behavior are methods of control. (2) The only choice we have is between methods of control that occur unconsciously or implicitly and those that are conscious and explicit. (3) It is preferable for control to occur explicitly and deliberately. (4) Therefore we ought consciously and deliberately to design and use methods of control to influence the behavior of others.

The argument is logically valid; the only issue is whether the premises are true. One prefatory point before I turn to an examination of the premises. Some of the criticisms I shall be making are relevant only to those who propose changing behavior by methods associated with the idea of "behavior modification," but other criticisms will apply to those who believe that deliberate changes are, by that fact alone, superior to leaving things to unplanned change (quite independently of the modes of change that are favored).

ARE THE PREMISES TRUE?

Premise (1) can be understood as making a verbal or substantive claim. Anybody is free to adopt a scheme of classification according to which any method used by one person to influence the behavior of another is a form of control. On this view if I want to influence you to meet me at noon I can ask you to do so, I can offer you $1,000 to do so, I can threaten your children if you do not meet me, I can promise you a stimulating conversation if you come, and so forth. All of these will be (by definition) ways in which I (try to) control your behavior.

But beyond the verbal issue of what *words* we use to label various methods of influence is a matter of substance. Understood substantively, (1) makes a claim that the various ways in which we

4 B. F. Skinner, *Beyond Freedom and Dignity* (New York: Knopf, 1984), 163–75.

151

influence one another do not differ significantly along an important dimension. The dimension in question is that of methods of influence which interfere with or restrict autonomy and freedom and those which do not. The substantive claim is that the methods used to influence others do not differ sufficiently in terms of their impact on freedom to be worth distinguishing some of them as methods of control.

The first thing to note about this claim is that analyzing notions of control, persuasion, influence, and so forth is not a task that is independent of one's theoretical convictions concerning the science of human behavior. If one believes, as Skinner does, that all behavior is shaped and maintained by its consequences, that all causal influences come from the environment, that when we seem to turn control over to the person we are simply shifting from one mode of environmental influence to another, that it is in the nature of an experimental analysis of human behavior that it should strip away the functions previously assigned to autonomous creatures and transfer them one by one to the controlling environment, then it will seem compelling to think of all ways of influencing people as merely different forms of control. The only moral issue becomes that of finding less aversive and more effective controls.

On the other hand, if one believes that any adequate explanatory scheme for human behavior must make appeal to mental states of one kind or another, that in many cases the working of such inner states are affected only marginally by the environment, that a research strategy which ignores the existence, and possible efficacy, of such internal states has proven barren in the past (and there is no reason to expect it to prove more viable in the future), then it will seem compelling to want to make distinctions between various ways of influencing people – distinctions which reflect what our best available theories tell us about the way the mind works.

To make this more concrete, consider Skinner's discussion of a key concept with respect to the issue of control – persuasion.

We also seem to be acting upon the mind when we *urge* a person to act or *persuade* him to act . . . We *persuade* people, however, by pointing to stimuli associated with positive consequences . . . We persuade someone by making a situation more favorable to action, as by describing likely reinforcing consequences.[5]

5 Ibid., 93.

If we use Skinner's definitions of reinforcement (a consequence of behavior that makes the behavior more likely to occur again), we see that to persuade someone is to describe consequences that are likely to have the effect that the person does whatever he is being persuaded to do again. But it is clearly not enough simply to describe some nice thing and claim it is a consequence of the behavior in question. Whoever is being persuaded must be brought to believe that the nice things are indeed consequences of the behavior, that there is a connection between the behavior and the consequences, that other nonnice things will not also occur, and so forth. How does one do that? By making a good argument, or pointing to evidence, or reminding someone of something, or whatever we do when we seek to convince somebody of some truth. Thus Skinner's analysis of persuasion itself depends on an understanding of what it is to follow an argument.

As to his view that "changing a mind is condoned by the defenders of freedom and dignity because it is an ineffective way of changing behavior, and the changer of minds can therefore escape from the charge that he is controlling people,"[6] this will depend on the nature and content of the particular arguments. If I point out to you that the bridge over which you are about to drive has collapsed, this is a very effective way of changing your behavior.

Even if I do describe facts to you as part of an effort to persuade you, these need not be reinforcing consequences of a negative or positive kind. If I point out to you that Goldbach's conjecture has never been proved, you might get interested in the problem and buy a book on number theory. Surely a statement of the historical fact about a theorem in mathematics cannot be taken as a reinforcer of the act of buying books. Of course, if we understand by reinforcement the things we already understand by "taking an interest in, getting excited by, wanting to learn more," then we can save the theory, but it adds nothing to what we already knew.

So far we have seen the relevance of certain views about the nature of psychological explanation to the issue of analyzing various modes of behavior control. Skinner could still be correct in his view that all modes of influence should be assimilated under the rubric

6 Ibid., 97.

153

of control. All I have argued so far is that his particular arguments for that view depend on controversial, and in my view mistaken, ideas about the nature of psychology.[7]

VARIETIES OF INFLUENCE

What kinds of distinctions might we want to make between various ways of influencing people? I use "influence" as a neutral, generic term for any way in which we can get people to change their beliefs or behavior. At the crudest level, we might want to distinguish between reasons and causes. I might get you to jump in either of the following ways. In one case I go up to you and challenge you to jump a certain distance. You accept the challenge and you jump. In the second case I sneak up behind you and yell in your ear "JUMP!" And you jump. The difference between the two cases is obvious. How to analyze it, and whether the analysis of the second case (which is just a reflex action) will carry over to other cases supposed to be instances of causes rather than reasons, is not at all obvious.

Philosophers have made finer distinctions within the category of changes involving reasons. For example, they have distinguished a class of incentives, and concentrated on two distinct categories – threats and offers. Behavior modifiers make a similar distinction under the heading of aversive versus nonaversive techniques or negative versus positive reinforcers.

Political philosophers have worried about whether freedom is affected differentially by threats and offers. By "freedom" here one does not mean a notion of free will in the metaphysical sense, but the ordinary contrast between those actions done voluntarily and those one is forced to do. It was crucial for philosophers in the liberal tradition to argue that only coercion interferes with freedom (liberty), not the offering of rewards or positive inducements. For if it were thought that transactions entered into for the prospect of gain could be unfree, then the ideological defense of the market economy, the idea that trade takes place freely when both parties view their positions as improved by trade, is threatened.

---

7 For further discussion of this issue, see Noam Chomsky, "Psychology and Ideology," *Cognition* 1(no. 1, 1972).

In addition to the political motivation there was a philosophical puzzle that bothered people. If one thought of a person as acting freely when he did what he wanted to do, when he did what he desired, then why should threats be thought to deprive people of freedom? If a robber says to me, "Your money or your life," and I hand him my money, didn't I do what I wanted to do? I could have refused, but I thought I would be better off acting as he commanded. So I did what I wanted, and I acted freely.

The solution to this problem is the following.[8] In order to understand why acting for certain reasons is interference with freedom and others not, one cannot just look at the actual situation in which the agent acts. Once faced with a robber there is no way of distinguishing between what the agent really wants to do and what he is forced to do. One has to step back and look at the second-order desires of the agent – his views about his motivations in the situation he faces. Does he mind acting for these particular reasons or not? People resent acting merely in order to retain a status quo against the interference of another agent (threats). They, normally, do not mind acting for the reason that they will improve their situation contingent on their accepting the terms of another agent (offers). To determine, therefore, whether acting for certain kinds of reasons is to be regarded as interfering with the freedom of the agent, we must inquire into the agent's second-order preferences as to acting for different kinds of resons.

Another way of looking at this issue, due to Robert Nozick, is to think about the agent's preferences for being faced with certain choices. Other things being equal, rational agents would not make the choice to be faced with the kind of choices that a robber presents them with, but would choose to be faced with the options that, say, an attractive offer poses. So we determine whether the agent is free by looking at the "metachoices" that he would make.[9]

Notice how if these accounts are correct a methodological approach to the explanation of behavior that denies the existence of

8 Gerald Dworkin, "Acting Freely," *Nous* (November 1970), 367–83. Cf. Harry Frankfurt, "Freedom of the Will and the Concept of a Person," *Journal of Philosophy* 68 (Jan. 14, 1971), 5–20.
9 Robert Nozick, "Coercion," in P. Laslett, W. G. Runciman and Q Skinner, *Philosophy, Politics and Society*, fourth series (Oxford: Oxford University Press, 1972), 101–36.

"inner" mental states is precluded in principle from making a distinction between methods of influence that interfere with freedom or autonomy and those that do not.

It is clear that there are a lot of different distinctions that we make in this area: A distinction between creating reasons for action and calling attention to reasons that already exist – compare threats and warnings. A distinction between processes of influence that bypass any appeal to reasons at all and those that work via reasons – compare argument and drugs. A distinction between cases in which the reasons being appealed to are made explicit and those in which they are used covertly – compare a legal brief and subliminal advertising. We certainly do not have a unified theory that can give a rationale for all these distinctions, and there may be none, but neither Skinner nor others have given us a reason to show that either these distinctions cannot be made or that there is no significant point in making them.

I conclude that the first premise is not true, or at least that we have no reason to believe it to be true. I now want to assume, for the sake of argument, that it is correct. Suppose that none of the ways in which we influence people differ significantly along the dimension of control. Is it the case that, therefore, we ought consciously to design and implement patterns of control as opposed to letting the existing methods continue in an unplanned and unconscious fashion? Is the third premise true?

ARGUMENTS AGAINST DESIGN

The general form of the claim is familiar from other contexts. It is often claimed, and quite correctly, that the failure to take certain kinds of actions does not result in nothing being done but rather in allowing the status quo to retain its current shape. Failure to intervene in various situations results in the continuation of the existing pattern of forces and their resulting effects.

In addition (3) appeals to our sympathetic attitudes to doing things explicitly and consciously rather than in a concealed and unplanned manner. It is often argued that most social science research contains various normative assumptions, and rather than concealing them under a false label of value-free social science it is preferable to admit that such assumptions are inevitable and to make

156

them explicit. In this way the social scientist can be made aware of possible sources of bias, and others can criticize the assumptions and replace them if necessary.

There is the further point that in the case of behavior control we may be able to accomplish our ends more effectively if we deliberately set out to modify behavior rather than have such changes take place on a hit-or-miss, random basis.

Given these plausible considerations one can understand why the premise is often taken as obvious or uncontroversial. But if there is no such thing as a free lunch, there is also no such thing as a cost-free policy. Being conscious and deliberate has its own costs as well as its benefits. What are some of these costs?

One set of costs are decision-making costs. Whenever we have to think about, plan, deliberate about, and evaluate our actions, there are costs of time, energy, money. To design a house is quite different from moving into one that we find abandoned or that is built for other purposes. To design a culture (a chapter heading in Skinner's book *Beyond Freedom and Dignity*) is going to involve a series of deliberations that are very extensive and an expenditure of time and energy that is enormous compared to accepting the results of the evolution of a culture. Now this objection is not very weighty, for if all else were equal we should surely choose to bear such costs. If the house I were to design were aesthetically more pleasing, more energy-efficient, functionally superior, and cheaper than a house I found, it would be worth a lot of time and energy spent in making decisions.

The next set of costs is more significant. These are the positive gains that can arise from serendipity, accident, chance. Suppose, for example (a not too far-fetched example), someone were to argue that too much scientific research takes place on a hit-or-miss, trial-and-error basis, according to principles of which we have little understanding, and often on an unconscious level. We would be better off, she says, if we tried to understand what the principles underlying scientific discovery are and then make conscious use of them. But, like the centipede who became incapable of locomotion when he tried to understand how his legs moved, this might be the very worst thing to do in terms of promoting scientific discovery. Of course whether or not self-consciousness impedes or promotes any particular goal is an empirical question not to be settled by a priori methods. But we do have enough examples of cases in which matters are worsened rather than improved to let the case for self-consciousness go by default.

The above considerations apply to the means we use to achieve specified goals, for example, understanding the laws of nature. But the more significant issue concerns the ends we ought to pursue. Premise (3) assumes that we can have better, sounder knowledge concerning the goals of behavioral change by making the processes of influence more deliberate and conscious. This is not at all obvious. It is very unlikely that by using deliberate processes we can think of all the possible candidates. Allowing a "random generator" to throw up various candidates, from which we can, as a result of observation and experience, weed out the bad and retain the better may actually be more efficient.[10] It is helpful to think of evolution in this connection. Imagine what creature might have been produced by a deliberate decision to fashion a person, as opposed to the process by which random mutations occurred and natural selection retained those modifications that had survival value and rejected those that did not.

A different point concerns the specificity of the desirable states that we ought to bring about. The premise of the superiority of deliberate design assumes that every goal can be specified in advance in a concrete fashion. This underlies the therapeutic practice of establishing "contracts" with clients before the therapy begins. But many of our ends are such that they are recognized as valuable only after they have been experienced – the I-know-one-when-I-see-one phenomenon. Again I have no firm views as to the percentage of our ends that have this character – although I believe the percentage is not insignificant – but the point is that if *any* desirable goals have this character they cannot be achieved by deliberate planning (which by assumption depends upon our having identified desirable ends in advance).

There are also values, such as spontaneity – of letting things happen as opposed to deliberately bringing them about – which run counter to the idea of conscious deliberation. These are valued, at least in part, not because they contribute to other ends (such as efficiency or the avoidance of responsibility) but for their own sake.

10 For further discussion of this point, see Robert Nozick, *Anarchy, State and Utopia* (New York: Basic Books, 1974), 312–17.

Think, for example of those parents who, if offered the possibility of determining the sex of their children, would decline. In the case of sex-selection, as in the case of behavior control, I do not deny that the opposite choice may be equally rational or better. I am only questioning the assumption that the decision favoring spontaneity must be the inferior choice.

It is also important to see that the decision for conscious planning means that we would have to regard the world in general as a rather different place than we do now. If all our interactions with others were to be thought of as being the result of conscious and deliberate thought (or as even *possibly* the result) – if not necessarily at the moment then at least at some earlier stage – the experience of the world would take on a very different character. (Think of the old joke of one psychiatrist passing another and saying "Good morning." The second psychiatrist says to himself, "I wonder what he meant by that.") Now it is true that in such a world we don't have to think this way (questioning motives and intent). We could decide that it would be better to retain our old attitudes, that failure to do so would lead to paranoia. But the point is that we are always faced with the possibility of such questioning and that possibility no longer can leave things in just the way they were.

Now it might be thought that my argument is unfair in the following sense. Premise (3) should not be interpreted as the assertion that design is always superior to nondesign but rather as the weaker assertion that, other things being equal, it is superior. But I have intended my considerations to count against the weaker interpretation as well. The claim that deliberate interventions are, *caeterus paribus*, superior to nondeliberate ones is equivalent to a claim about where the burden of proof should lie. On the view being examined it should lie on those who favor the status quo of many unconscious and unintentional influences rather than those who propose to make more change intentional. While I do not argue for a view (such as Edmund Burke's or Michael Oakeshott's) that deliberate change is always likely to be worse than what the wisdom of past experience has taught us, and therefore that the burden of proof should always be on reformers, neither do I accept the opposite position. It seems to me that there is no general presumption here. The considerations adduced in favor of putting the burden of proof on one side are evenly balanced by considerations leading the other way. Only by looking at particular modes of influence, in particular contexts, given a specific body of knowledge, with a particular set of persons, and a specific set of goals, can we reach a reasonable decision. There are no general principles, not even ones assigning a burden of proof. There is no general argument that gives would-be controllers a head start.

Epilogue

I am well aware that these essays represent the middle of a research program rather than its completion. In the past few years a number of books have been published that have made significant contributions to this effort.[1] I shall outline some of the problems and issues that require continued investigation.

There are a number of conceptual issues that must be worked out in greater detail. Perhaps the most crucial is gaining a better understanding of the difference between what I call "procedurally independent" second-order evaluations and those that are not. Roughly, the distinction is between those modes of evaluation that interfere with the rationality of higher-order reflection and those that do not. We believe, prior to philosophical reflection, that there is a difference between a person who is influenced by hypnotic suggestion or various modes of deception and those who are influenced by true information and modes of rational inquiry. In the former case, but not the latter, we think of someone else as responsible for his reasoning and his conclusions. This is not a metaphysical distinction but a practical one and it is important to make explicit what criteria we use to make such a distinction.

It would also be useful to work out the connections between a clearly defined notion of autonomy and other notions such as rationality, being free, self-knowledge, ambivalence, neurosis, weakness of the will, and so forth. The tendency in the literature has been to suppose that all good things go together, and so an autonomous person will (or must) be virtuous, nonneurotic, rational, and so forth. My own inclination has been to try and sharply separate autonomy from other capacities and character traits, while

1 Lawrence Haworth, *Autonomy: An Essay in Philosophical Psychology and Ethics* (New Haven: Yale University Press, 1986). Robert Young, *Personal Autonomy: Beyond Negative and Positive Liberty* (The Hague: Croom Helm, 1986). Lawrence Crocker, *Positive Liberty* (The Hague: Nijhoff, 1980).

acknowledging that there may be contingent connections, which range from some of these other conditions being part of the process of developing or promoting autonomy to such conditions being more likely to be present in autonomous persons.

In this connection there is a task that philosophers have relegated to social scientists – who have responded by ignoring the issue. This is to speculate about what psychological and social conditions are likely to promote the development and maintenance of autonomous individuals. The excuse given by philosophers is that this is an empirical question about which they have no claim to expertise or knowledge. But what I am suggesting is not that philosophers assess the evidence for or against various hypotheses but that they *suggest* types of inquiry. Whether Plato, Aristotle, or Mill were correct about the social conditions they thought were required to develop various types of character is not up to philosophical inquiry to determine. But their reflections are valuable as guides to the kinds of empirical inquiry it would be useful to pursue.

There are also a number of evaluative and normative questions concerning the value of autonomy that require further investigation. Questions of paternalism will always be with us but I believe that the general theoretical questions have by now been well explored and that the most fruitful way to make further theoretical progress is by more detailed studies of particular, concrete areas where the issue arises. I think here of the controversy that continues to grow about the attitude of the society toward smoking, or the issue of whether to allow surrogate mother contracts when one has reasons to believe that some women will find it psychologically damaging to give up the child they bear, or those interventions, such as antisuicide measures, that are designed to preserve the possibility of autonomy for the agent.

An issue that has received relatively little attention is the conflict between what might be called individual and group autonomy. Consider a community that is oriented around a set of common values. These might be religious in nature (Mennonites) or ideological (Owenites) or moral (pacifist) or even aesthetic. Such a community may perceive, correctly, that allowing individuals in their midst to adopt very different values and ways of living may be incompatible with the full flourishing of their own values. It is simply not sufficient for those who support certain values to live in accordance with them without regard to how others are living.

162

To take an extreme example consider a monastic order that imposes vows of silence. It is not sufficient for members of the community who value silence to refrain from speaking to each other. If silence itself is valued then this can only be achieved, so to speak, collectively. We have a conflict between the desires of a community to live in accordance with their autonomously chosen values and the desires of individuals who, in the exercise of their own autonomy, choose to reject or ignore such values. How ought the legal and social systems respond to such conflicts?

A similar issue arises with respect to the set of issues that have been discussed under the heading of the enforcement of morals. Assuming there are immoral acts that do not cause what might be called *secular harm*, under what circumstances is a majority entitled to interfere with such acts by coercive means? It is clear that such interference is an infringement of the liberty of the person being interfered with, but the traditional liberal assumption has been that as long as there is no harm to other individuals or the community as a whole, there are no grounds for restriction of such activity. But why isn't it a good reply to this argument to assert that members of the majority have ideals which they are trying to promote (say that of chastity) and for others to act in ways counter to those ideals is to harm such ideals either directly, or by encouraging others to deviate, indirectly. If a person has certain ideals in terms of which she defines herself, say, chastity, why is she not harmed by constant exposure, in the flesh or in media, to distractions and temptations? Why may she not seek protection against those who act in ways that publicly disparage her ideals and encourage others to undermine them? This issue has traditionally been discussed under the heading of the limits of liberty. As I have argued, the two concepts are not equivalent and arguments from autonomy, the capacity to define the kind of person who wants to be, may give more weight to the arguments in favor of the enforcement of morals than traditional liberal thought has done.

Another empirical question to be studied is what kinds of communities would be favored by individuals who pursue the exercise of their autonomy as a central aim. I have claimed that there is no intrinsic tension between autonomy, as I conceive it, and communitarian values. Nevertheless it may be the case, as a matter of contingent fact, that individuals who place great value on their autonomy will be less likely to form communities that are based on the promotion of communally held values. Is a stress on individual autonomy corrosive to communitarian values?

There is another set of questions that have been usually discussed with respect to liberty but that may take a different shape when discussed with respect to autonomy. These are questions about the regulation of individual economic activity by market mechanisms. Ideological disputes between libertarians and socialists have often taken the form of disputes as to whether "liberty" is a "negative" or "positive" concept. In the recent literature the debate has been shaped by Robert Nozick's argument that attempts to protect a given pattern of income distribution (which is regarded as desirable) will require that persons be prevented from doing what they freely and knowingly choose to do.[2] The argument goes on by claiming that even if such acts create patterns of inequality that lead to some persons having to work for others this does not involve restrictions on the liberty of the "proletarians."

However if we turn to a notion of autonomy that involves people being able to shape their own lives in important ways, not being subject to the influence and power of others over important parts of their lives (even when such power does not take the form of coercion), then significant inequalities may reduce the likelihood that individuals will exercise their autonomy. If individuals are made aware of this fact, and fully appreciate the long-run consequences of their actions, they may be less likely to exchange the short-run pleasures of watching Wilt Chamberlain for the long-run losses in control over their lives. More generally the traditional socialist concern with equality may be seen as guided by an instrumental interest in the maximization of autonomy.

This brings me to my final item on the research agenda. It has been fashionable in moral philosophy in recent years to separate consequentialist moral theories into a value theory and a maximization principle. Consequentialism is defended against critics of utilitarianism by avoiding a one-dimensional pleasure-based value theory. One can have a rich value theory, it is argued, that has other values such as justice, self-realization, equality, respect for persons, and so forth. What remains essential to consequentialism

2 R. Nozick, *Anarchy, State and Utopia* (New York: Basic Books, 1974), pp. 161 ff.

is that whatever the good is, the right consists in the production of as much of it as possible. This is simply rationality as applied to practice. One drawback with this view methodologically is that it gives up the great virtue of utilitarianism, which is that as a single-valued theory one could assess the good without having to consider tradeoffs among distinct values. Once we introduce multiple values, such as liberty, equality, *and* welfare, then many of the most difficult moral problems simply transfer over to the value theory. Although I do not think that the maximizing view is the correct one, those who wish to defend it *and* are dissatisfied with multiple goods *and* reject traditional welfarist theories of the good may find it more promising to see what consequentialism would entail if there were but a single good – autonomy.

Finally a word of warning about the relation between theory and practice. Work in applied ethics has assumed a familiar pattern. First the practical issue is spelled out in some detail and the moral issues are raised and clarified. Then various factual matters are spelled out and speculations are made about the possible consequences of various alternative resolutions. Next, fragments of some theory are displayed; usually some variant of utilitarianism or social contract theory. Finally, the theory is applied in fairly mechanical fashion to the set of facts, and some normative conclusion is asserted to follow from the theory. I have sometimes thought of writing a software program called Ethicon, which essentially provides the outline for the resolution of any moral issue by following the above steps. Different versions could come with different theories – EthiKant, EthiRawls, EthiMill, and so on.

I do not seek to add to the list. I do not think there are weightings that can be given to the value of autonomy that enable us to resolve conflicts of value in such a way that any rational person must agree. I do not view a philosophical theory as replacing moral and political conflict, but as providing a clearer picture as to what the conflicts are about, and indicating where those who accept such a theory take their stand, and the ideal of a person and society they advocate. If proponents of such theories are fortunate they may be able to convince others of the attractiveness of their ideas and ideals. Even so the step from theory to practice is not usually deductive. Sometimes it will be clear that a certain resolution of a moral dilemma is literally inconsistent with a certain value or ideal or conception of the person. But, most often, the relation will be more like what action best expresses that ideal, or what attitude best reflects this conception of the person, or what rules cohere best with the values that underlie this institution. What to do may be theory guided, but not theory determined.

Bibliography

Ackerman, Bruce. *Social Justice in the Liberal State* (New Haven: Yale University Press, 1980).

Aiken, Henry. *Reason and Conduct* (New York: Alfred A. Knopf, 1962).

Anscombe, E. "Authority in Morals," in *Concepts in Social and Political Philosophy*, ed. R. E. Flathman (New York: Macmillan, 1973).

Arrow, Kenneth. "Gifts and Exchanges." *Philosophy and Public Affairs* (Summer 1972).

Berlin, I. *Four Essays on Liberty* (Oxford: Oxford University Press, 1969). *Two Concepts of Liberty* (Oxford: Clarendon Press, 1969).

Buchanan, A. "Medical Paternalism." *Philosophy and Public Affairs* 7 (Summer 1978).

Burke, Edmund. "The English Constitutional System," in *Representation*, ed. H. Pitkin (New York: Atherton, 1969).

Butler, Joseph. *Five Sermons*, ed. S. Darwall (Indianapolis: Hackett, 1983).

Capron, A. M. "Informed Consent in Catastrophic Disease Reasearch and Treatment." *University of Pennsylvania Law Review* 123 (December 1974).

Chomsky, Noam. "Psychology and Ideology." *Cognition* 1 (1972).

Crocker, Lawrence. *Positive Liberty* (The Hague: Nijhoff, 1980).

Deardon, R. F. "Autonomy and Education," in *Education and the Development of Reason*, ed. R. F. Dearden (London: Routledge & Kegan Paul, 1972).

Downie, R. S., and Telfer, Elizabeth. "Autonomy." *Philosophy* 46 (April 1971).

Dworkin, Gerald. "Acting Freely." *Nous* (November 1970). "Autonomy and Behavior Control." *Hastings Center Report* (February 1976). "Non-neutral Principles." *Journal of Philosophy* 71 (August 1974). "Paternalism." *Monist* 56 (January 1972).

Dworkin, Ronald. "Liberalism." in *Public and Private Morality*, ed. S. Hampshire (New York: Cambridge University Press, 1978).

Feinberg, Joel. "The Idea of a Free Man," in *Education and the Development of Reason*, ed. R. F. Dearden (London: Routledge and Kegan Paul, 1972). "Legal Paternalism." *Canadian Journal of Philosophy* 1 (1971).

Fingarette, H. "Punishment and Suffering." *Proceedings and Addresses of the American Philosophical Society* 50 (1977).

167

Frankfurt, Harry. "Freedom of the Will and the Concept of a Person." *Journal of Philosophy* 68 (January 1971).

Freeman, B. "A Moral Theory of Consent." *Hastings Center Report* (August 1975).

Fried, C. *Medical Experimentation: Personal Integrity and Social Policy* (New York: Elsevier, 1974).

Gert, Bernard, and Culver, Charles. "Paternalistic Behavior." *Philosophy and Public Affairs* 6 (Fall 1976).

Gewirth, A. "Positive 'Ethics' and Normative 'Science'." *Philosophical Review* 69 (January 1960).

Goldstein, Joseph. "On Being Adult and Being an Adult in Secular Law," in *Adulthood*, ed. E. H. Erickson (New York: W. W. Norton and Co., 1978).

Griffiths, A. Phillips. "How Can One Person Represent Another?" *Proceedings of the Aristotelian Society* 34 (Suppl. 1960).

Hare, R. M. *Freedom and Reason* (Oxford: Clarendon Press, 1963).

Harper, F., and James, F. *The Law of Torts* 68 (Suppl. 1959).

Hart, H. L. A. "Rawls on Liberty and Its Priority." *University of Chicago Law Review* 40 (No. 3, 1973).

Haworth, Lawrence. *Autonomy: An Essay in Philosophical Psychology and Ethics* (New Haven: Yale University Press, 1986).

Hill, Jr., Thomas. "Autonomy and Benevolent Lies." *Journal of Value Inquiry* 18 (No. 4, 1984).

Hume, David. *Treatise of Human Nature* (Oxford: Clarendon Press, 1888).

Kierkegaard, S. A. *Fear and Trembling and the Sickness Unto Death*, trans. Walter Lowrie (Garden City, NY: Anchor Press, 1972)

Kristeller, P. O. "The Philosophy of Man in the Italian Renaissance." *Italica* 24 (July 1947).

Locke, John. *The Second Treatise of Government* (New York: Library of Liberal Arts, 1952).

Lucas, J. L. *Principles of Politics* (Oxford: Oxford University Press, 1966).

Meisel, A. " 'The Exceptions' to the Informed Consent Doctrine: Striking a Balance Between Competing Values in Medical Decision-making." *Wisconsin Law Review* 79 (No. 2, 1979).

Mill, John Stuart. "Considerations on Representative Government," in *Three Essays* (Oxford: Oxford University Press, 1972).

"On Liberty," in *Three Essays* (Oxford: Oxford University Press, 1972).

Principles of Political Economy (New York: J. F. Collier & Sons, 1900).

Nozick, Robert. "Coercion," in *Philosophy, Politics, and Society*, 4th Series, eds. Peter Laslett and Walter Runciman (Oxford: Blackwell, 1967).

Oakeshott, Michael. *On Human Conduct* (Oxford: Clarendon Press, 1975).

Oppenheim, Felix. *Dimensions of Freedom* (New York: St. Martin's, 1961).

Parfit, D. *Reasons and Persons* (Oxford: Oxford University Press, 1984).

Peters, R. S. "Freedom and the Development of the Free Man," in *Education and the Development of Reason*, ed. R. F. Dearden (London: Routledge and Kegan Paul, 1972).

Pitkin, Hannah. *Representation* (New York: Atherton, 1969).

Rachels, James. "God and Human Attitudes." *Religious Studies* 7 (No. 3, 1979).

Rachlin, H. *Introduction to Modern Behaviorism* (San Francisco: W. H. Freeman, 1970).

Ramsey, P. *The Patient as Person* (New Haven: Yale University Press, 1970).

Rawls, John. "Construction and Objectivity." *Journal of Philosophy* 78 (September 1980).

"Kantian Constructivism in Moral Theory." *Journal of Philosophy* 77 (September 1980).

A Theory of Justice (Cambridge: Harvard University Press, 1971).

Royce, Josiah. *The Philosophy of Loyalty* (New York: Macmillan, 1908).

Scanlon, Thomas. "Contractualism and Utilitarianism," in *Beyond Utilitarianism*, eds. A. Sen and B. Williams (Cambridge: Cambridge University Press, 1984).

"A Theory of Freedom of Expression." *Philosophy and Public Affairs* 6 (Winter 1972).

Scitovsky, Tibor. *The Joyless Economy* (New York: Harper & Row, 1976).

Sellers, W. "Is Scientific Realism Tenable?" *Proceedings of the 1976 Philosophy of Science Association* 2, eds. F. Suppe and W. Asquith (1977).

Singer, Marcus. "Freedom From Reason." *Philosophical Review* 79 (April 1970).

Singer, Peter. "Freedoms and Utilities in the Distribution of Health Care," in *Markets and Morals*, eds. G. Bermant, P. Brown, and G. Dworkin (Washington, D.C.: Hemisphere, 1977).

Skinner, B. F. *Beyond Freedom and Dignity* (New York: Knopf, 1984).

Science and Human Behavior (New York: Free Press, 1953).

"Some Issues Concerning the Control of Human Behavior: A Symposium with Carl Rogers." *Science* 124 (November 1956).

Slater, Philip. *Earthwalk* (New York: Harper & Row, 1974).

Titmuss, Richard. *The Gift Relationship* (New York: Pantheon, 1972).

Toulmin, S. *Human Understanding* (New Jersey: Princeton University Press, 1972).

Tullock, Gordon. "Inheritance Justified." *Journal of Law and Economics* 14 (April 1971).

The Logic of the Law (New York: Basic Books, 1971).

Veatch, R. "Three Theories of Informed Consent: Philosophical Foundations and Policy Implications." *The Belmont Report* (Washington, D.C.: DHEW Publications, No. OS 78–0014, 1982).

Wolff, Robert Paul. *The Autonomy of Reason* (New York: Harper and Row, 1973).

In Defense of Anarchism (New York: Harper and Row, 1970).

Wolf, S. "Asymmetric Freedom." *Journal of Philosophy* 77 (No. 3), 159.

Young, Robert. *Personal Autonomy: Beyond Negative and Positive Liberty* (The Hague: Croom Helm, 1986).

Index

171

varieties of, 87–90
see also informed consent
consequentialism, 164–5
contractualism, 115
criminal sanctions, 141–4
Crocker, Lawrence, 81n

Dach, Leslie, 99n
Della Mirandola, Pico, 13
Descartes, René, 53
design
    arguments against, 156–9
    and costs, 157
DeTocqueville, Alexis, 11
Duhem, Pierre, 51
Dworkin, Gerald, ix, 19n, 75n, 76n,
    121n, 155n
Dworkin, Ronald, 3, 4, 10

English, Jane, 81n
entrapment, 130–49
    and Abscam, 145–9
    and creation of crime, 136–41
    and encouraging crime, 142–4
    as a legal defense, 133–6
    legitimacy of, 141–5
    and predisposition, 133–6
    and testing virtue, 144–5

Feinberg, Joel, 124
Fingarette, H., 143
Francis, Leslie, 129n
freedom (*see also* liberty), 23, 25, 152,
    154–6
Fried, Charles, 113

Goldstein, J., 94
Green, T. H., 105
Griffiths, A. Phillips, 90

Hare, R. M., 10, 34, 46, 49, 50, 51, 60
Hart, H. L. A., 9, 37, 75
higher-order reflection, 18–20
Hobbes, Thomas, 86, 105
Humboldt, W. von, 11, 29
Hume, David, 42

identification, 15–16, 20
independent judgment, 19, 27, 45, 56
indoctrination, 18
informed consent, 100–20
    and autonomy, 106
    exceptions to, 115–20

justifications for, 101–3

Kant, Immanuel, 5, 8, 10, 13, 26, 31,
    34, 36, 39
Katz, Jay, 103
Kierkegaard, Soren, 10, 34, 73
Kraut, Richard, 81n

liberty, 13–15, 18, 24–5, 30, 64, 95,
    121, 164
Locke, John, 14, 88, 105
loyalty, 23–4
Luther, Martin, 13

Mack, Eric, 129n
Macklin, Ruth, 99n
Marcuse, Herbert, 11
Marx, Gary, 145n
Mill, John Stuart, 11, 28, 29, 65, 92,
    93, 94, 105, 162
moral autonomy, 34–61
    and action, 41
    and authority, 42, 51
    formulations of, 34–5, 49, 57–8
    and judgment, 41
    and objectivity, 39–40, 47, 54, 57
    and obligation, 41–2
    and responsibility, 43–4
moral principles, 34–6, 49, 58
    being one's own, 34–8
    causal influences on, 38
    choosing of, 37, 50
    social character of, 36–7
    truth of, 58, 60, 61
moral reasoning, 59–60
motivation
    first-order, 15, 16, 19, 20
    higher-order, 15, 16, 18, 19, 20

Nagel, T., xiii, 60
Nietzsche, F., 10, 34
Nozick, Robert, 64, 155, 164

Oakeshott, Michael, 47, 159
objectivity, 58–60
    practical, 59–61

paternalism, 76, 106–7, 121–9, 162
    and autonomy, 123, 129
    and choice, 76
    definition of, 121–4
    hard vs. soft, 124–9
    justification of, 124–9
    and slavery, 125, 128

172

person
    conception of, 31, 32–3
    ideal of, 31–2
Pitkin, Hannah, 90, 93
Plato, 53, 162
Popper, Karl, 10, 34
Postema, Gerald, 145n
practical reasoning, 59
pro-active law enforcement, 130–3,
    135–7
procedural independence, 18–19, 21,
    29, 30, 161

Quine, W. V. O., 51

Rabinowitz, Joshua, 81n
Rawls, John, 3, 9, 30, 31, 40, 57, 58,
    60, 64, 74, 86, 96, 113
Reismann, David, 11
representation, 90–4, 95–7
Rousseau, Jean Jacques, 105
Royce, Josiah, 9, 10, 23, 24

Sartre, J. P., 34, 37
Scanlon, Thomas, 3, 26, 27, 60

Schneewind, J., 59n
Scitovsky, Tibor, 72
self-determination, 12–13, 95, 112
Sellars, Wilfred, 61
Singer, Peter, 70, 71
Skinner, B. F., 8, 152, 153
Slater, Philip, 73
Socrates, 86
substantive independence, 21–5, 28–30
substituted judgment, 91–2

therapeutic privilege, 118–20
Titmuss, Richard, 64, 70, 71
Toulmin, Stephen, 55
Tullock, Gordon, 63, 64, 69

voluntariness, 14–15, 124

Weinberg, Melvin, 145–9
White, Patricia, 145n
Wittgenstein, Ludwig, 67n
Wolf, Susan, 17
Wolff, Robert P., 3, 4, 10, 25, 26, 34,
    40, 42, 109

173